SINCLAIR

THE WORLD'S END MURDERS THROUGH THE EYES OF A KILLER

RYAN GREEN

Disclaimer

This book is about real people committing real crimes. The story has been constructed by facts but some of the scenes, dialogue and characters have been fictionalised.

Polite Note to the Reader

This book is written in British English except where fidelity to other languages or accents are appropriate. Some words and phrases may differ from US English.

Copyright © Ryan Green 2018

All rights reserved

ISBN-13: 978-1984031907
ISBN-10: 1984031902

For Helen, Harvey, Frankie and Dougie

CONTENTS

Introduction 7
Early Days 15
A Reformed Character 36
Frances Barker 44
Anna Kenny 48
Hilda McAuley 57
The World's End 65
Agnes Cooney 83
Mary Gallacher 89
Living in Fear 97
Cold Cases 109
Trial and Jeopardy 114
Conclusion 121
About the Author 127
Other Titles by Ryan Green 128

Introduction

It was close to ten o'clock, but the night was still young. Christine's heels were clattering on the cobblestones as she marched them down the Royal Mile to the last pub of the evening. The chill of an autumn night was being held off by the warmth of bodies in the city but even the gin in their stomachs couldn't keep the streets dry. Helen kept slipping on the cobbles, clinging to Christine's arm and cackling every single time her ankle almost turned. Both girls were swaying to distant music, still following them along from the last bar. Up ahead were the old gates to the city, now long worn away to nothing but a scattering of brass cobbles across the street. There used to be a warning up on those gates that there was nothing beyond them. That this street was at the end of the world. Helen's world didn't stretch much further than the end of the street at the moment either. She was wrapped in a cloud of warmth, laughter and an alcoholic haze. Her whole world wasn't much bigger than her and the echoes of Christine's heels.

Beyond that bubble of warmth, the city lay sleeping. The old town was still a hubbub of drunken antics and music, but further out the streets lay dark, damp and silent. For an instant, Helen's stomach turned over looking down that street into nothingness. It was always there, just out of sight. Even beneath their feet, beneath the cobbles that were ringing out the sounds of their passage, there were dark catacombs cut into the very stone beneath the city, capturing the strange echoes and calls from above and reverberating with forgotten secrets. For a moment, Helen's steps faltered, the smile slipped from her face—for one awful moment she felt the darkness pressing in all around her and the cold slipped in past her defences to send a shiver up her back. Then she heard it. The door to the pub swung open and the song pulsed out, wiping that moment of realisation away in a flood of giggles. The song had been following them from pub to pub all along the mile. Christine started to sing along, 'Yes sir, I can boogie...'

Helen collapsed into another fit of giggles in her friend's arms, trying to join in as they swayed towards the inviting glow of the pub and the billow of blue smoke that escaped each time the door was opened. They shimmied through the door together cracking up as they tried to sing: 'If you stay it can't be wrong...'

They had to wait in the doorway for a long moment as a group pressed out, heading to one of the dozen other pubs in spitting distance, or heading home from the way that some of the girls were melting in the men's arms. There was a pair of girls with the very same dresses on as Christine and Helen. Their hair was practically the same too. All four of them froze in place looking at their doppelgangers, then they burst out laughing and moved along. It was a small world with only a few shops where you could get a cheap dress to wear out on a Saturday night—this was hardly the first time this had happened. They were lucky to have a night out when one of their friends wasn't wearing the same dress. It wasn't strange enough to even remember once they were through the door and enveloped in the cigarette smoke and music. There was an atmosphere in the World's End that you couldn't find anywhere else on the mile. The pub was older than radio, the staff knew every one of their regulars by name. It felt like home in a way that the other pubs didn't. At seventeen, Helen and Christine hadn't been going to pubs for very long but of all the ones that they had tried, this was probably their favourite. The crowd wasn't much different from the usual Saturday night, a hundred and fifty people crammed in until you barely had room to move for all the elbows. They were starting to trickle out now that it was getting closer to closing time, so the girls had to push against the flow of bodies to get to the bar and get a drink. The crowd was like a living, heaving ocean that could dash you against the rocks if you fought it or part around you gently if you knew how to swim through it. In the swirl of faces it took them a few minutes to find a familiar landmark, and even when they found their friends there wasn't enough room at their table, so they were forced to linger, brushing up against the crowds as they moved through. Helen made her way to one of the raw stone walls, a relic of the old city that had somehow survived the centuries. She leaned her head back against it and let the cool steady presence of the stone seep into her and calm the spinning in her head. The music wasn't as loud in here as in the other pubs. The World's End was where you came to wind down at the end of the night or to get something decent in your stomach at the beginning. It was a little island of peace in all the chaos of a Saturday night on the town. A drunk in a leather jacket dashed past her towards the bathroom making retching noises. Peace was a relative term.

She only had a moment to calm herself before her friends Toni and Jackie pushed through to get her attention, Christine following along at their heels looking hopeful. Toni leaned in close enough to be heard over the hundred conversations around them, 'Alright, hen?'

Helen gave her a smile and a nod. She was already a little hoarse from all the smoke in the last three pubs and didn't want to yell over the racket in here without good cause. Toni came even closer, the tang of cider on her breath. 'We're going along to a party next, do you two want to come too? Should be some fit lads. Some dancing.'

Helen chuckled. 'Sorry love, I'm knackered, this is the end of the line for me.'

Christine clucked. 'Might get your second wind yet.'

'Maybe next time, eh?' Helen demurred.

Toni rolled her eyes and grabbed Jackie by the arm before she could become a stick in the mud too. 'Yeah, maybe. See you later.'

The boy in the leather jacket came past again in Toni's wake, trying to smile at them and just looking nervously queasy. The girls collapsed into giggles before he was out of sight. Christine had to lean on the wall too, to keep from falling under the weight of her laughter. Between gasps, she choked out, 'What is wrong with men?'

Helen put her face in her hands. 'I swear...'

From beyond the protection of her fingers, she heard a rumbling voice. 'Can I buy you drink?'

Christine burst out laughing all over again, but Helen managed a coy smile before waggling her full glass at the poor guy. His shoulders were already slumped in defeat. She tried to soften the blow.

'Maybe later, eh?'

He was mumbling as he backed away, but that brought a little smile to his face and he gave her a cheeky wink before vanishing into the crowd. In about five minutes Helen would forget what his face looked like, and he would probably have found some girl who was thirstier. Christine hooked her arm through Helen's elbow and dragged her off the wall. 'Come on hen, I'm not standing around all night.'

There were a lot of familiar faces in the crowd—some of them were friends, some were just such a regular feature in the nightlife of Edinburgh that their absence would have been noted, and once in a while, there was a boy in the crowd who had spent the night flirting with them. One of the disposable men that they might have kissed or might have just smiled at, men who had been forgotten about by Sunday morning. Near the back of the bar by the public telephones, they found themselves a table for two that had just been abandoned. There was still a cigarette butt smouldering in the ashtray, marked around its filter with scarlet lipstick. Christine stubbed it out along with her own and they settled in for a chat. Back here it was quieter and most of the heavy flirting was happening around them. Everywhere you looked there were hands resting on bared knees and the couple at the table in the corner were probably going to be chucked out before they were arrested for being indecent in public. The girls took it all in with a giggle and enjoyed each other's company. They had been best friends since they were in school and even without the social lubricant that they were sipping, the conversation had always flowed easily for them. A pair of men sidled up to their table before long and here in this warm and happy place, it felt perfectly natural to chat with them. One of them had his hair cut short, and he had patches on his pockets that made Helen think he was a builder. The other one, the one who couldn't keep his eyes off Christine, had a big black moustache like Burt Reynolds. They were older than the boys that you usually met on a Saturday night, more mature and confident. That self-assurance and the fact that they weren't too painful on the eyes was enough to win Helen over. The men bought them their drinks and they chatted away happily with them until the bell rang for last orders. All the tiredness that had been dogging Helen's steps along the Royal Mile had faded away, just as Christine predicted, and she found herself feeling sorry that the night was over, feeling a pang of regret that she hadn't taken Toni up on her offer of a party. The drinks had been flowing steadily since they arrived, so she was happy to take a hand up when it was offered to her. The radio had cycled around again and 'Yes Sir, I Can Boogie' was playing once more. The girls wiggled their way across the room, arms flailing, and heads thrown back through the chorus. The crowd parted around them with a rippling wave of laughter and the men, their dates, couldn't keep amused expressions off their faces. Christine wrapped her arms around Helen and they both boogied their way out the door.

They made their exit with all of the same grace with which they had arrived in the World's End. Christine tripped and stumbled as they came out of the pub, saved from landing face down in the gutter by one of the policemen who patrolled this stretch of town at closing time for pretty much that express purpose. She thanked him profusely and he handed her back into the waiting arms of the man behind her. 'What do you say girls, shall we give you a lift home?'

Helen chewed her lip. 'I'm not sure.'

'We'll take you anywhere you want to go.'

Christine met her gaze and Helen let her happiness get the better of her. A smile spread over her best friend's face as she said, 'Oh go on then.'

They headed off down St. Mary's Lane with their arms linked, still laughing at some stupid joke from the bar. Both of them chattering, warm and filled with so much life it was practically overflowing. Why shouldn't she take a lift from a couple of nice guys? It wasn't like she was going alone, Christine would keep her right, even if they had both had a bit too much to drink. They had nothing to fear and everything to look forward to. After all, they had their whole lives ahead of them.

Early Days

The Second World War had wrought death and destruction on the world on a scale that was unimaginable, and one month after it came to an end in Europe the true atrocities that had been committed were still being uncovered. It would take the world decades to come to terms with the evil that had been done, but for many people, this was considered a time of great hope. The war was over and now a new peace could be forged, a lasting peace that would persist through the rest of humanity's time on this planet. Many babies were born in 1945 as a resurgence of hope spread around the world and people started to rebuild. How ironic that one of those babies of hope was Angus Sinclair.

Angus Senior and Maimie Sinclair lived in Glasgow. Angus Junior was their third child. They had resided in a tenement flat on St Peter's Street in Glasgow for over a decade and they were well known in the local community. Angus Senior was a joiner from Stirling who was often called on to help with odd jobs in the block. Maimie came from a long line of miners, the first of her clan to migrate to the city with hopes of a brighter future than lungs full of coal dust were likely to provide. Glasgow in the post-war years was far from the bright and bustling metropolis of today. You could not see six feet away from you thanks to the cloying smog, and the tenements where the Sinclairs lived were densely packed fire traps where the poor of the city were hidden from more civilised eyes. Despite Angus Senior's much needed manual skills and ceaseless hunt for work, the family were always on the edge of starvation but for the ongoing rationing ensuring that they got the minimum they needed to live. Despite that, Angus was a happy child, playing with his older siblings and the children in the street. The lack of nutrition stunted his growth, so he was always the smallest child his age, and he wasn't well liked among the rough and rowdy neighbourhood children, mainly being tolerated for the sake of his brother and sister.

When Angus was four things took a turn for the worse. His father had been getting more and more tired and worn down over the course of the last few months, and while the family assumed it was caused by his work hours and the sudden cutback in available food after rationing was ended, the doctors disagreed, diagnosing Angus Senior with chronic leukaemia. For the next two years, Angus Senior weakened and withered, losing his job, spending more and more time in bed and eventually becoming Maimie's full-time responsibility. She nursed him through the final two years of his life as the illness stole any trace of vitality from him and left him as little more than a living skeleton. Young Angus watched all of this without a word, although his mother would later claim that he missed his father terribly in the years that followed. His concerns were less mortal and more practical at the time. He had been attending Grove Street Primary School, directly opposite his tenement, for over a year by the time his father died and during that time he had not made a single friend. He was relentlessly bullied for being the smallest in the class, for being a little bit slower than his classmates and, ultimately, for his poor social skills. His older sister Connie was something of a social butterfly, but Angus became introverted and quiet in the face of the abuse until eventually he barely spoke at all.

The people from his street and the tight-knit local community came to recognise his strangeness but attributed it to his unfortunate family circumstances. It would not be until later that they recognised the signs of the burgeoning monster living amongst them. Even his family ignored his increasing detachment from the world, with his mother still describing him as a 'good boy' until he started to attend secondary school several years later. When he became a teenager, he began to go through the usual changes that puberty brought, but when his sexual appetites began to develop, they had no healthy outlet. All of the boys picked on him and all of the girls ignored him. He became fixated on sex as a cure-all for his unhappy and unsatisfying life and his fantasies became more and more violent, focused entirely on dominating and punishing the girls who wouldn't give him a second thought. In school, he was a failure both in his studies and in his social life, with one of the teachers bluntly describing him as being 'not a simpleton, but of below average intelligence.' In his frustration with life he began to act out, and at the age of thirteen, he had his first brush with the law.

Maimie trudged to the door, weighed down by the laundry of three perpetually filthy children. The all-too-familiar triple knock of the police came again. She let out a sigh and dumped the armful of washing onto the bed. She wasn't even surprised when she saw Angus between the two policemen, just resigned. 'What's he done this time?'

After a second of silence, one of the police rapped his knuckles off the back of Angus' head. 'He was caught stealing ma'am. Nicked the offerings box right out of a church.'

Angus grumbled, but a quick slap around the back of his head silenced him again. He scowled furiously at his mother's feet. The policeman prodded the boy forward. Angus was sporting a black eye. 'We won't be pressing any charges, but if we catch him at it again there's going to be more trouble than a wee whack will fix.'

Maimie's breath caught in her throat. 'He's no getting charged?'

The policemen glanced at each other and shrugged. 'It's a Catholic church. Once the Fenians got their money back they didn't care. But we won't forget about this anytime soon. That boy needs to get his head sorted or it is going to go very badly for him.'

Angus still didn't say a word. He tugged himself free of the policemen's grip and brushed past Maimie on his way into the house. She had tears in her eyes as she mumbled her thanks. This time he wasn't going to jail, but he was only going to get so many second chances.

The robberies were just the tip of the iceberg, and while Angus was caught once or twice for breaking into the flats in the local area and ransacking them for valuables, the levels of crime in the tenements were so high that it was hard to assign the blame to a single thirteen-year-old boy when there were dozens of equally likely suspects. The fact that so many of the break-ins were happening in such close proximity to Angus' home made the police overlook him as a suspect. Not only was he a needle in a haystack, he was also breaking from the known pattern of criminals in the poorest areas of Glasgow at the time. Crime had always happened, but there were strong communities in the tenements, and even the lowest petty criminal didn't prey on their own people. On the few occasions when he was caught, Angus was given a swift beating and sent home. Criminal proceedings were a lot of trouble, and while Angus was a nuisance to the local police, he was mostly beneath their notice with so much real crime going on. Every time he got away with another robbery, his confidence grew along with his belief that the police would go on overlooking him. With that newfound confidence, he began pursuing his lifelong goals.

He quit school, withdrawing from everyone in his peer group entirely and cutting himself off from anyone his own age. For his mother, it was a mixed blessing: on the one hand, he was cutting himself off from any chance of advancing in life, but on the other, he was now able to start contributing to the household. He got a job as a van boy and began earning a paltry wage at the age of fifteen. More importantly, the job got him out of the house and away from the closes where he lived. Even before turning to crime Angus had been intensely unpopular, but now he was at risk of being attacked just for walking down the street, and he had neither the intelligence to diffuse the situation nor the physical strength to defend himself. He rode around in the back of a van, loading and unloading for the owner, and gradually he learned the lay of the land outside of the tiny corner of Glasgow where he had spent his entire life.

Cowcaddens was near to the centre of Glasgow, another council housing estate like the one that Angus called home. It was far enough away from his usual haunts that he was not immediately recognisable but not so far that it felt like unfamiliar territory. He passed through it frequently when he was working, and one day when he was finished for the day he walked back through those smog-shrouded streets and spotted a little girl of about eight years old playing alone, completely unattended and completely unaware.

It isn't clear what lie he told her to make her go into the nearest close. He had not had years of experience to help him develop his usual performance revolving around a lost dog, or an errand needing run that he would happily pay for. Regardless, he tricked the girl into the close, followed her inside, pinned her against the wall and molested her for his own twisted pleasure while she screamed and cried. Once he had satisfied himself, he left her lying in the stairwell and headed for home. This time when the police came knocking at his door, it was not to administer a slap on the wrist. His mother thought that he was being taken away for another small-scale larceny like he had committed so frequently through his teenage years, and he did nothing to destroy that illusion. She remained one of the few people who he believed were on his side and he did not want his ravenous sadistic and sexual appetites to be revealed to his mother.

Because of his age, Angus could not be tried as an adult or sent to prison. The judge administered the harshest sentence that he could for a first offence, recognising the callous disregard that Angus had for the damage that he had done to a child. The boy was sentenced to three years on parole, with any further offences resulting in jail time. The case was kept quiet to prevent an outbreak of violence from the family and community of the victim. Angus returned home, returned to his job and returned to the strange equilibrium of his solitary life. His family did not turn on him, although his oldest brother was already living elsewhere and may not have been informed of the gruesome details. Instead, they maintained the lie that Angus was a perfectly normal boy, that his youthful exuberance had gotten him into trouble with the law. The old lie that 'boys will be boys' came back, again and again, to protect him from the consequences of his disgusting actions. He remembered every detail of his crime, and he used those memories not only as fuel for his sexual explorations but also to refine his process. He recognised early on in the case that the only evidence the state truly had against him was the eyewitness testimony of the little girl whom he had made his victim. He realised that if he could silence the victim then his terrible actions might go entirely unreported. He did not have the presence, intelligence, charisma or finesse to intimidate his targets into silence, so he instead opted for the simplest way to silence a victim. A method that coincidentally fit in perfectly with his increasingly violent urges.

Catherine Reehill had lived in the impoverished closes of Glasgow for all seven years of her life, but that was soon coming to an end. Her parents had left her and her siblings in the care of their numerous aunts and uncles while they travelled to London to seek out accommodation and work. They had big plans for a brave new future at the other end of the country, an escape from the slums that had defined their lives until now. Catherine was too young to have had anything to do with the children of the Sinclair family, her neighbours, but she was old enough to recognise them as local fixtures.

The temperature had been climbing all week and now it was so hot that spontaneous fires had lit up several of the closes around the city, rendering dozens homeless. The newspapers called this time the 'Glasgow sizzles.' Trapped within the shadowy flat he called home, Angus was pacing restlessly. His sister and mother were out. He had just turned 16 a few weeks ago. Since he had been placed on probation, he had not dared to act on any of his darker impulses. Even the small relief of breaking and entering would have condemned him to years in prison. The heat was oppressive, and he felt like he couldn't breathe, trapped in the stuffy little flat while the world outside burned. Even if the weather had been reasonable he would have been pinned in place by the constant whispering of his neighbours. They didn't know what had happened to that little girl in Cowcaddens and they had no right to judge him. It wasn't his fault that girls his own age weren't interested in him. If one of the wee bitches at school had given him the time of day, it wouldn't have come to this.

He could have gotten what he wanted without all these unwanted consequences. It wasn't fair that he got the blame for everything all the time. They were just mean to him. They were bullies. He stalked over to the window, wiping sweat out of his eyes. Wee Catherine from the next close over was skipping along the pavement like you couldn't fry an egg on the concrete. Her skirt flipped up every time she hopped, and he caught a glimpse of the pale skin that the sun hadn't tanned. Angus tried to wet his lips, but the heat had dried out his tongue until it felt like a lump of leather in his mouth. He gulped some cold water straight from the tap, then ran back to the window. Cathy wasn't wandering far, just skipping back and forth along the road. Whoever was meant to be looking after her while her parents were away had obviously told her not to wander too far. They were trying to keep her safe. To say that he made an impulsive decision when he saw that little girl skipping up and down the road would have been a lie. He moved around the flat rapidly, gathering together the things that he needed and laying them out. Last, he scooped a penny out of the jam jar of savings that he had been putting aside from his job and headed down the stairs.

'Cathy,' he mumbled. The little girl didn't hear him over the sound of her own rhyme and the slapping of her feet. Angus looked up and down the street. There was nobody else around, so he took a perilous step out of the shadow of the building.

'Cathy, come here a second.'

The girl stopped and stared at him. He was still short, and the bulk that years of manual labour would pile onto him hadn't even begun to emerge yet. Angus looked closer to her age than his real sixteen years. Young enough that any vague warnings about talking to strangers faded from Catherine's memory. She was too young to recognise his nervousness as anything except funny. The sweat dripping from his face could be attributed to the heat without much stretching of the imagination. When he gave her the penny and asked her to bring him a bar of chocolate from the shop down the road, it didn't even occur to the child that there was anything out of the ordinary. She bought him his chocolate, and a bar for herself as that had been the price he had agreed for her running this errand, then she hiked back along the street. She took one last look up at the clear blue sky and the blazing sun before she stepped into the refreshing shade of the close. She walked into the darkness without looking back, anxious to get up the stairs before her chocolate could melt.

At the door to his flat, she handed over the chocolate and his change, then he invited her in and she politely declined. He tried once more to persuade her. 'Come on, it's roasting out there, your chocolate will melt.'

His predatory nature must have shone through because the girl tried to run. He caught her by the arm. When she tried to tug free he smacked her with the back of his hand. Blood started to pour from her nose, staining streaks down the front of her sundress and leaving a polka dot pattern in the dust of the close floor. The blow stunned her just long enough for him to drag her inside and slam the door shut.

Inside the flat with nobody around, all the pretence of humanity fell away. He grabbed her by the hair and dragged her screaming into his room, then he tossed her down onto the bed. She cried out 'Daddy! Help me!' as Angus dragged her skirt up and climbed on top of her. Her screams turned from fear to agony as he molested her, and her supplications for help echoed through the flat, so loud that Angus was sure they would be heard. He could not afford to be caught. Not again. It would be jail for sure this time, and jail wasn't kind to sick little boys who liked to hurt little girls. He would be lucky to get out alive. This girl knew him. There was no possibility that she wouldn't go running to the police at the first opportunity. If he wanted to stay free, he would have to take that opportunity away from her. He fumbled one of his bloodied hands up over her mouth to keep her quiet and fumbled down the side of the bed with the other, eventually pulling his final piece of preparation out: a makeshift ligature made out of the inner tube of a tyre. He wrapped it around her throat and pulled it tight. The skin around the pinching point turned an angry red, but it wasn't enough. He twisted the tube in his hands, dragging it in tighter and tighter until the rubber was biting into the little girl's neck all around. Like it would only take one more twist to tear the whole thing off. He knew that he wasn't meant to enjoy this part. He knew that this was just meant to be for his protection so that she couldn't go crying to her mummy and daddy and all the police in Glasgow about the bad boy from next door. But as she bucked and flailed around beneath him he realised that this was as good as sex. This was better. He pressed himself down on top of her and continued to pull on the tyre. She shuddered as he squeezed the last drops of breath and life out of her and he had never been happier.

Afterwards, he stared at the dead little girl on his bed for a solid minute before he became aware of the passage of time. He went to the bathroom and cleaned himself up with a washcloth. He tugged her clothes back into place as best he could and then he carried her out into the hall. He was suddenly intensely aware of how many people were just behind those doors, hidden out of sight and ready to pop out at any moment. The people in this building didn't hate him any less than the people in the street, or the kids at the school across the road. They would love to catch him out like this. He dragged the girl down two flights of stairs as quickly as he could. He nearly had her out the front door of the close when thought better of it. The basement stairs were right there, as good an excuse for her death as any. He pulled her over to the steps and weighed it in his mind. She had fallen down the stairs. She fell down the stairs, officer. Tragic accident. He nodded and then threw her limp corpse down the flight of stairs with a smirk. It wasn't perfect, but who was going to look at it twice. Little girls had stupid accidents, that was life, especially here in the housing schemes.

He scrambled back up to the flat, ready to start scrubbing away any evidence that had been left behind. It was bad enough having to deal with all the scum out there, but if his mother turned on him it would all be over. There wasn't much, except the inner tube that had been stretched completely out of shape, the perforated rubber looking wet where it had cut into her. He shoved it down to the bottom of the bin then returned to his room and made his bed before tossing his clothes back on top of it. Everything as it should be. He heard footsteps in the hall and panic welled up. What if they found her? What if the shouting started now? He wasn't ready yet. He hadn't prepared a story in case the police came. What if someone had seen him giving the girl money? He would need to admit that he had seen her. He would have to act like he was annoyed that she had run off with his penny. That would work. He could beat this. All that he had to do was stay calm and collected. All that he had to do was not freeze the way that he did when he was trying to talk to girls. What could be easier than lying to the police? It was almost second nature to him. But he needed time. He needed time to think.

Without that time, he made rash decisions, he burst out of his flat and ran down the stairs, trying to catch up to the mystery footsteps. All that he had to do was make sure they didn't see her. He could distract them if he needed to. He could... There was a scream from the foot of the stairs. He skidded down the last few steps, trying not to trip himself. There were two old women standing with their hands over their mouths, looking down into the basement. He panicked and blurted out, 'I'll call the ambulance.' The women mumbled something, but he was already out in the street, running for the bright red phone box at the end of the road. He dialled the operator and got through to the ambulance service in moments. He fumbled over his lie, eventually blurting out: 'Catherine fell down the stairs. There is a little girl. She fell down the stairs in a close. She isn't breathing.'

He ran back to the close before the ambulance could arrive. Only one of the old women was still there. He told her the ambulance was coming then ran back up the stairs again. In the flat, he locked the door and slumped to the floor. That was stupid. He had drawn attention to himself. There was no way the old biddies downstairs weren't going to recognise him. The police knew his name, they knew his face. They were going to pin this on him no matter what he did. He stuffed a change of clothes into his sports bag and left.

The police catching up to Angus was the best thing that could have happened to him. Catherine was declared dead in the ambulance on the way to the hospital and it did not take the medical staff long to realise that most of her injuries had occurred after her death and the ones before it were not consistent with a fall. The police in London scoured the boarding houses of their city looking for her parents to report the terrible news. Her uncles had taken to the streets to hunt for Angus before the sun had even set. His molestation of another young girl had been the gossip of the street for months and he had been spotted at the scene of the crime. It didn't take much to put two and two together. If the Reehill family found Angus, they planned to kill him. The police were not able to force a confession out of Angus. He stuck resolutely to his version of events despite all the circumstantial evidence arrayed against him. In the early hours of the morning, he was picked up by the police several miles away in the centre of Glasgow, wandering around on foot. It is entirely possible that he would have walked away from the grisly crime if it wasn't for the intervention of his older brother John, who convinced him that a confession was the best course of action. Inside jail, he would be protected from the fury of the Reehill family, and if he confessed then his sentence was likely to be much lighter than if he fought the case all the way. Knowing the truth of the situation and suspecting how much of his story could be proven false very easily, Angus followed his brother's advice. It would be the last time that the boys spoke to each other. After convincing Angus to throw himself on the court's mercy, John wanted nothing to do with his brother ever again. He was charged with his crimes in the old Patrick Marine police station as soon as it opened for business on Monday morning. Catherine's parents arrived in Glasgow to identify the body at about the same time.

This time he was old enough to be tried as an adult and, given the horrific nature of his crime, the courts were more than willing to throw the book at him. His mother came to visit him while he was still on remand and all of the empathy that he denied others came flooding out now that he had been caught out. He wept to his mother. 'Why did I do it? Why did I do it, mother? Why did I do that to her? I've caused that little girl's parents so much grief, I've hurt them so bad. I don't understand. Why did I do it?'

At the time, the cold and calculating manner in which he had planned and committed his crime was not known to the court. It was only decades later when his true nature had been revealed to everyone, when it was no longer to his advantage to lie, that all of the details came out. Psychiatrists were brought in to evaluate Angus. One of them described his behaviour after committing what should have been a disturbing action as so mundane as to be considered abnormal. He had treated the act of disposing of a corpse, inventing a false narrative and constructing a fake crime scene as no more unusual than taking out the rubbish. It indicated that something was fundamentally wrong with Angus. Further testing determined that he had an IQ of no more than 80. It was not low enough for him to be considered developmentally disabled, but it was taken into account by the court that he may not have understood the significance of his actions. In response, another psychiatrist brought in by the court stated, very clearly, that Angus had a psycho-sexual disorder and that for as long as he was alive, he would continue to commit sexually motivated attacks. The psychologist recommended that Angus should be permanently separated from society for the protection of the general population. The court took the combination reports to mean that Angus was mentally impaired, and therefore not as culpable for his actions. In light of it being his first offence as an adult and the overblown remorse that he acted out while pleading guilty, he was sentenced to only 10 years in prison.

On his first day inside, Angus was expecting violence. The population of Saughton Prison in Edinburgh wasn't just made up of the local thugs and hooligans. People from all over Scotland were imprisoned there, and that meant that at least some of the dozen people from his patch of Glasgow who had been jailed over the last few years would be in there with him. If he could get away with a beating, then he would consider himself lucky. For the first time, he was afraid. He had to cough every time he tried to ask a question during his induction to the facilities to cover up the fact his voice was cracking. Every person that he passed was staring at him, and he just knew that the story about the boy who had murdered a wee girl was already doing the rounds. They would come for him in the night when the guards weren't looking, or in the showers. Maybe they would stab him in the cafeteria while he was waiting for his dinner, bodies pressed in on either side of him, nowhere to run, nowhere to hide. They would get caught if they killed him in public, but some of these lads were in here for the rest of their lives anyway—it would make their lives easier if they got a reputation for killing scum like him.

It was like his worst nightmare. Like living in his street in Glasgow, except the walls of his flat had been pulled down and all the people that hated him were able to see right inside. Or at least, that was how he imagined it was going to be. Angus might have been the main character in his own story, but to the prisoners, he barely even registered as existing. Even if someone on the outside did wish Angus harm, all letters coming into the prison were checked and censored to maintain order. After the first few days, older prisoners took him under their wing and his confidence began to grow. By the time that his mother and sister made their first visit, he was as happy as they had ever seen him. Regardless of how Maimie and his sister Connie interpreted what had happened on the fateful day that Angus killed a girl, it was the last straw for his older brother, who had watched the runt of the litter that he had tried to protect from the bullies of the world turn into a monster before his very eyes. John never spoke to Angus again for the rest of his life. For their mother, seeing Angus happy and healthy in jail gave her a new lease on life.

She immediately began laying plans for his future; preparing paperwork that would let him change his name and giving consideration to emigrating when his ten years of imprisonment were over. She was ready to uproot herself and her whole family for Angus, but it was a small sacrifice. They may have lived in the same place for a long time, but any connections that they might have made to the community had been firmly severed by his crime.

He spent the next six years behaving like a model prisoner. A social circle of the Glaswegian criminals accepted him on its fringes alongside the other sex criminals who would become his closest friends and mentors in the prison. In those years prisons did not only pay lip service to rehabilitation. Angus was taught a trade as a painter and decorator so that he would be able to re-join society after he had served his time. In the seventh year that he was in prison, he was given day release to go and work with decorating companies in Edinburgh, to learn the fine details of the trade in an abridged apprenticeship. Unfortunately, he was also learning a second trade from his new friends. In prison, he traded notes with other sex offenders and they refined their techniques. Angus learned how to cover his tracks, how to act confident in the face of questioning and how to charm his victims instead of relying on brute force. Whatever delusions his mother might have entertained about starting a new life didn't take the reality of her son's obsessions into account. After his seventh year in prison, after showing exemplary behaviour throughout his stay, he was released early.

A Reformed Character

Maimie's plans to migrate away from Glasgow never came to fruition, in no small part due to Angus' complete lack of interest in fleeing. His time in prison had taught him a little bit about how big the world was and how little it cared about individuals. He did not need to hide away or change his name. If he walked down a street as if he owned it, then people would assume that he belonged there. He assumed the disguise of a perfectly normal man of his age in stages. First, he found himself a regular paying job with one of the firms in Edinburgh who had finished his training, then he settled into a flat of his own within the city, out from under his mother's watchful eye. A flat similar to the one he had grown up in, only a stone's throw away from the World's End pub and the Royal Mile at the heart of old Edinburgh.

The next stage of his plan for normalcy was more difficult to coordinate because it involved not only assuming a mask of humanity but maintaining it, day in and day out. It took him almost a month to muster up the courage to start dating, not because of any fear of rejection, but because of the commitment that it was going to require. He met his future wife, Sarah Hamilton, in a bar on one of the few nights out that student nurses were allowed. He didn't have to layer on much charm to persuade her to be interested in him. The years had given him time to fill out his short frame, and he was considered by most women who met him to be fairly attractive by the time he was twenty-five. Sarah lived in nurse's accommodations attached to Edinburgh's Eastern General Hospital at the time, so it took little to persuade her to move in with her new lover, and in a fairly short time, the two of them were ready to tie the knot.

At a small ceremony in the registrar's office in Leith, the two of them made their vows in front of both of their families. While Angus' older brother refused to attend, Sarah's younger brother Gordon, then aged fifteen, was excited to spend some time with his new brother-in-law, a man he looked up to and considered to be the pinnacle of cool. Angus' kind sister and her husband had given him a place to stay when he first came to Edinburgh, and they served as witnesses to the ceremony. Maimie was overwrought with emotion, completely delighted that her son was back on the right track to a happy, normal, life. They did not talk about his time in prison or the terrible event that had sent him there. Both Gordon and Sarah knew that Angus had spent some time behind bars, but that only added to his appeal. They had no idea what he had done.

The pair honeymooned for two weeks in Campbeltown on the Kintyre peninsula, where Sarah was impressed once again with the intensity of Angus' affection and attention. The two of them explored a little of the area, with Angus claiming to be scouting for fishing spots, but they spent the vast majority of the trip in their hotel room. On the outside, they appeared to be very much in love, in the throes of passion, but so much of Angus' energies came from a place of darkness rather than genuine care for another person. He had Sarah captive on their honeymoon, with no distractions, and he made use of the outlet that she provided. Sarah saw his constant pawing as a good sign, an indicator that they were going to have a healthy relationship, when his nymphomaniacal fixation on her body was actually a symptom of a deeper-rooted problem. One that would come back to haunt the family again and again through the years.

Between the two of them, the new Sinclair family were doing well for themselves. Angus had gone into business for himself and was reaping the benefits of his labour directly, and Sarah was working steady shifts at the hospital. They were starting to accrue some savings and were able to move into a bigger flat together—the future was looking bright for both of them. Once Angus was confident that the marriage was secure, he began to do some pre-emptive damage control with Sarah. He sat her down a year into the marriage and explained that he had been sent to jail for killing a child. She was horrified but he already had a web of lies prepared to keep her under control.

He made sure that he was her only source of information about his crime, and he framed the story to make it seem like the killing had been accidental rather than deliberate. Sarah's brother Gordon had been in considerable trouble with the police when he was younger, so she was familiar with the idea that people make mistakes when they are young. He played to that, and combined with the idea that she already knew him so well apart from that single incident, it was simple enough for her to put it out of her mind. He was careful never to tell her an outright lie, but he gave her enough vague information for her to form her own, more flattering picture of what had happened. If anything, this 'show of trust' on his part, in telling her about this horrible thing from his past, served to strengthen their relationship—which was going to prove vital to his plans in the near future when his mask of normalcy was all that stood between him and convictions.

Following the work, the couple moved to Gallowgate in Glasgow, staying with the family of one of Sarah's older brothers. Maimie became a constant presence in their lives and Sarah grew closer to her mother-in-law. They formed a support network for the young couple that would become essential when, two years into their marriage, Sarah gave birth to their first and only son, Gary.

Maimie was delighted that Angus' life was back on track, and she absolutely adored Gary, doting on him and spending every moment that she could helping out. With her support, Sarah was able to return to work, and before long the couple had more money than they knew what to do with. Angus was able to invest in an ice cream van to supplement his painting income, and not long after that he purchased a campervan, which he would use to take his brother-in-law Gordon on 'fishing trips'. He developed an interest in photography but would not let anyone see his pictures. He was so devoted to the privacy of his work that he set up his own darkroom rather than allow a professional to develop his pictures for him. Angus had constructed the illusion of a perfect life, and his new cheerful personality seemed to reflect the idea that he had become a normal person. He drove around the neighbourhood in his ice cream van, stopping to sell children and their parents his wares. He smiled down at little girls the same age as his first victim every single day, isolated and alone on the street with him, in easy reach of his grasping hands, and he sold them treats.

Sarah was so completely content with her life that she was able to ignore the little niggling doubts about Angus that were starting to arise. Rumours crept their way back to her that his weekend 'fishing trips' actually involved bar hopping and loose women, but her brother was happy to corroborate any story that Angus told her, so it was difficult to doubt him. He was having almost constant affairs during those years, and on rare occasions, Sarah's friends were able to catch him in the act and report it back to her. He instantly began begging for forgiveness and swearing that he would never be unfaithful again, as if a switch had been flipped in his head. He was using all of the women as an outlet for his sexual obsessions, Sarah included, but between their conflicting schedules and his voracious appetites, she was never available to him as much as he wanted her to be. He would pick up women in bars with Gordon as his wingman and they would have sex in the campervan that was purchased for that purpose and rarely parked far away. This still wasn't enough for Angus. Sex and violence were intrinsically linked in his psyche, and he was not finding the satisfaction that he had hoped for in his consensual affairs, no matter how sordid. Just as he had when he was a child, he turned to crime as a way to get his blood pumping.

There was a string of violent muggings across Glasgow. Angus did not wait for his victims to offer up their property, opting instead to attack first and snatch whatever valuables he could from their unconscious bodies afterwards. He caved in one woman's face with a claw hammer before snatching her purse. He pounced on a man from behind, hacking at him with a hatchet before stealing his watch and his wallet. While his declared income on his tax forms continually decreased and he worked less and less frequently, he never seemed to be lacking in funds. One of the criminal endeavours that he had never expected to prove so talented in was the creation of pornography, but partnering up with an elderly photographer in Dumbarton known locally as 'Wee Eddie' Cotogno, he was able to secure a steady income by tricking and coercing girls into posing nude for the old man.

The girls in Dumbarton had all been warned about the 'dirty old man', but the charming Sinclair, plying them with drinks and massaging their egos, found it much easier to convince them to take a few saucy snaps. Eddie preferred to take pictures himself, but when Angus couldn't find young women willing to submit themselves to his lecherous gaze, he would pass the camera off to the younger man and simply buy the negatives instead, assuming that they were of a high enough 'artistic standard'. In addition to satisfying himself with this hobby, Eddie was one of the steadiest suppliers in Scotland's underground pornography ring, catering to tastes that were a little more adventurous than could be met by the magazines of the time. He would sometimes get special requests passed back along the grapevine that he would then pass along to Angus. Scenes that might offend even modern sensibilities, or specific combinations of appearance and situation that could not be found elsewhere. Because the content they were producing was underground, they did not have to concern themselves with laws about the age of consent or obscenity. It was lucky for Eddie that he had found a complexly amoral but charming man like Angus to do his dirty work. It is unlikely that he could have met nearly as many of his 'special orders' if he was working alone. He was certainly happy to pass along the financial gains that he had made as a result to Angus. The money flowed out of the pockets of some of the richest and most perverse men in the country through a series of brown envelopes and directly into the waiting hands of Angus Sinclair.

Angus was even able to put down a deposit on a brand-new house for the family not long after this new crime spree began. Violence had always been an enjoyable experience for Angus, but now he was making it into a means to an end. But he was becoming dissatisfied with keeping his two passions separate. Violence and sex were two sides to the same coin for him, and while he had done what he could over the years to keep them separated, it seemed almost inevitable that he would eventually return to his one true passion. His marriage had been living on borrowed time, just another diversion to keep him from unleashing his true cruelty on the world again, and it was failing in that task rapidly.

Frances Barker

Frances Barker came home from visiting her sister in the early evening after a long day at the City Bakeries. The taxi driver dropped her off outside her flat on Maryhill Road and then drove away. A few buildings down the road, Maimie Sinclair was currently living with her son Angus and his family, who were there to keep an eye on her due to a bout of ill health.

Frances was thirty-seven years old, but wrinkles had barely begun to appear on her heart-shaped face, and her dark hair still hadn't lost any of its lustre. She was tired after a full day of work and a playful visit with her young niece, but she wasn't ruling out the possibility of a quick drink at her local pub before settling down for the night. When Angus, younger than her by a few years and ever so charming, pulled up beside her in his campervan, it didn't take much persuasion to convince her to take a lift and get a drink. This weekend Angus had left Gordon behind, taking an actual fishing trip on his own before returning to the city, so Frances sat in the front seat beside him while he drove them out of town. To begin with, she was startled at the change of plans, but a little bit of flirtatious chat soon had her convinced that they were going out to some country pub where Angus' wife wasn't as likely to hear reports about his seedy conduct with the lady next door. Frances had never found love in her life, flitting from one unfulfilling relationship to the next before accepting the welcoming arms of her sister's family as a substitute for children of her own. It had only been a few years since her last fling, so she was fairly certain that she knew how this was meant to go. She had no intention of getting caught up with a married man despite his charm. After a few drinks, if he tried to get fresh, she would just ask him to take her home.

He parked abruptly by the side of the road and dragged her out of her chair and into the back where he already had a bed made. When she tried to object he shoved her over and started to wrestle her trousers down. When she resisted him, he put a hand around her throat and squeezed until her hands lost their strength. He wasn't a huge monster of a man, but Frances was completely unprepared for his ferocity. After a few fumbling attempts to get them unbuttoned he ripped her trousers off her. He was breathing heavily and as awful as it was, Frances could at least console herself with the thought that it would be over quickly. He forced her legs apart with his knee and climbed on top of her, but she kept on clawing at him until he eventually snatched a spindle of string from under the bedcovers and bound her hands. Frances squeezed her eyes shut and tried to ignore the feeling of his hands on her bare skin. Tried to ignore him as he mounted her, as he grunted and drooled. His hands stopped roaming under her clothes and she considered it a blessing until she felt the rough press of rope across her neck.

He wrapped a knotted length of string around her throat and pulled with all the strength that his awkward leverage would provide, still thrusting and flopping on top of her as he tried to choke the life out of her body. It wasn't enough. The world faded to grey and there was a sound like the ocean roaring in her ears, but he wasn't pulling hard enough to kill her. She could still feel him on top of her. Inside her. She must have let out some sound because he seemed to realise that the ligature on her neck was too loose. For one glorious instant, he was off of her and his grip loosened. Frances could breathe again, and in a wash, all the disgust that had been withheld along with oxygen came flooding back. She tried to retch, tried to vomit all over him but her crushed throat was too swollen to let her. He came back and pushed himself back inside her before she could get a proper breath to fight him off. He pressed his whole weight down onto her and gathered the ends of the string in his hands. It drew tight enough to cut into her. Her eyes bulged, and she made one final effort to force him off, but all the strength had been stolen from her. He pulled the string taut and arched his back with one final lethal thrust. Blessed darkness took her, and she didn't have to endure another moment of his touch. He had finished some time in the midst of all that. Somewhere between the first cut of string into flesh and the jerk.

After taking a couple of minutes to clean up, Angus got back into the driving seat and rolled on down the road towards his usual fishing spot out by the village of Glenboig in Lanarkshire. He trussed up her body, still half naked, and then tossed her into a copse of bushes at the side of the local lover's lane, where she wouldn't be discovered for sixteen days, by which time almost all of the evidence that could have been found on her body had been contaminated by the local wildlife.

The police leapt on the case, and within a month they convicted a young man and known rapist called Thomas Young of the crime. Angus followed the story in the newspapers in the months that followed and couldn't believe his luck when the police searched Young's flat and discovered a makeup compact that Frances had received as a gift from a friend. Young eventually died in prison, still protesting his innocence, after his final appeal had been rejected by the Crown Court.

Anna Kenny

On Friday nights, the Hurdy Gurdy pub in Glasgow's Townhead was overflowing with bodies. It was sometimes described by the locals as a meat market, with men and women heading in to pair off with anyone who would have them for the night, but Anna Kenny and her friend Wilma Sutherland weren't interested in romance, they were just out for a night on the town after a hard week's work at the brewery. Anna had recently turned 20, and adult life and all its responsibilities were just starting to catch up with her. She had never felt tired before, sleepy sometimes, but not the bone-deep exhaustion that comes with a whole week of non-stop work. She had never been a heavy drinker and she would have thought that the stink from the brewery would have put her off booze for life, but she was learning how vital it was to relax at the end of a workday so that you could get a decent night's sleep and be ready for the next one. Two young men approached them in the bar, one of them younger than her and the other one a bit older, with a nice thick moustache that made her think of her dad.

He was so relaxed compared to the younger guy that she found herself gravitating towards him despite herself. He was a bit older but not so much that it felt gross when he gave her knee a squeeze under the table. More than anything, she felt safe sitting beside him. He wasn't obviously trying to get into her pants like his friend was doing to poor Wilma. He was laid back. If something happened, then it happened; if it didn't then he wasn't going to be pushy. It was like he already knew how the night was going to end so he didn't have to worry about it. He bought them a round and when he came back his arm settled comfortably around the back of her seat. Anna didn't even think about shoving it off. It felt good to have that warmth behind her. When the bartender rang the bell and declared the last call, the guy didn't jump on her or get weird, they just headed out the door.

Like a gentleman, he offered her his arm, and she couldn't think of a good reason not to take it. She said goodbye to Wilma, who the other guy was still desperately flirting with, and her gentleman agreed to walk her to George Square, where she could catch the bus home. Wilma went off in the other direction, looking for a cab so she could get away from the creep who had latched onto her. He was telling her that he grew up just along the road, as if that would impress her, when they went around the corner and out of sight. Anna almost stumbled as they walked along Lister Street but the guy, Angus, wrapped an arm around her and supported her. The streets were quiet, and the first chill of autumn was in the air, so she was glad of the company—otherwise, she might have been spooked. They were just walking past a parked campervan when he drew her to a halt. She had hoped that she could catch her bus without this awkward moment, but she already had her speech prepared: 'Listen, mate, I've had a lot of fun tonight, but I've been at work all day and I'm knackered. I just want to get home for a kip. Nothing else. Alright?'

Angus smiled at her, that calm easy smile he had been wearing all night. He said, 'Hey pal, don't worry about it. I'm not going to make you do anything you don't want to.'

He leaned closer and she turned her head away from his kiss, only to realise a moment too late that he was just reaching across to unlock the campervan door. He said, 'Look, I've only had a couple, how about I drive you home? Save you the bus fare?'

She was already blushing from her last misunderstanding. She didn't think her dignity would take another hit. 'No thanks, I've got my day ticket.'

He took a gentle hold of her arm before she could step away. 'Come on love, I'm really enjoying your company. I'm sure you won't even take me out of my way.'

She didn't feel the fear yet. The drinks all night had dampened down whatever instincts she had developed in her 20 years of life. It still felt like a conversation. "I'm no being funny, I'm just heading home. You're no getting to neck me in the car. You're no going to get anything from me. You understand?'

He held up his hands and laughed. 'I'm just offering you a ride. No funny business. Scout's honour.'

She let out an unladylike snort at that. 'Aye, I can just see you in a scout's uniform.'

He stuck out his tongue and pulled the door open for her and she climbed in without a second thought. The smile slipped from his face the moment her back was turned. He wouldn't need to wear that mask for much longer now.

Once the engine was on he went through the motions of asking where she lived. He even went to the bother of heading in that direction until she was lulled half to sleep by the gentle rocking and quiet music. By the time she realised they were heading the wrong way they were almost out of town. She pointed it out to him and he kept his jovial expression locked in place. 'Sorry love, I think I've made a wrong turn. Give us a minute and we'll get back on track.'

Ten minutes later she came out of her stupor enough to realise something was wrong. There was a shrill edge in her voice when she said, 'I don't even recognise any of these streets. Where are you taking us?'

He tried to shrug it off again, but Anna wasn't letting him off so easily. 'Oh, that's your game is it, drag me off to the middle of nowhere and try it on? To hell with that. Let me out here. I don't care where we are, I'll walk. Let us out.'

His smile flickered. 'I can't go abandoning you in the middle of nowhere now, can I? Let us find the main road and we'll get you back in no time.'

The chill realisation of the situation that she had blithely walked into settled in her guts like a cold weight. She shouted, 'Let me out of this bloody car. Right now.'

In the blink of an eye, his smile vanished, and the fatherly, cheerful expression contorted into something else, something base and predatory that tugged at the hindquarters of her brain and made her want to run. 'You aren't going anywhere, you mouthy wee bitch. Just shut up and sit still.'

She scrambled to unbuckle her belt and her hand was on the door handle before he said another word. It wasn't quite fast enough. His hand slammed into her chest, pinning her to the chair. He took her breast in the palm of his hand and crushed it through her shirt until she squealed. 'Shut your bloody mouth or you'll get a lot worse than a wee squeeze.'

She started to cry. The nice man she had left the pub with had transformed in an instant—all of Angus' daily deceptions dissolving away as easily as a normal person would change clothes. There was a monster in the seat beside her. A cold, calculating monster who had worn the skin of a man to get close enough to strike. When her sobs turned to howls, a cruel sneer crept onto his face. He took a grip on the front of her shirt again and twisted it, ripping it off her body as she struggled and wailed. Outside there was nothing but darkness; all the lights of the city had vanished around the same time that he had revealed himself. All that she could see were the road markings flashing by down the middle of the road and the hint of the moon behind the dense clouds. There wasn't a sign of another human being anywhere. His fingers ran over the bared skin of her stomach and she shuddered and hunched up in the chair, trying to get away from him. He started braying with harsh laughter as they sped around a bend, and her naked shoulder pressed against the cold window, making her jump back towards him.

He pulled off the road onto a short dirt track that ended abruptly at the gate to a field. The campervan bounced over the deep ruts in the mud and Anna was flung about without her seatbelt. The moment they stopped she went for the door again, but he caught her by the tattered remains of her shirt and dragged her back into the campervan. In the back was a bed and beside it, he had laid out some lengths of knotted rope. He had been planning this from the start. He had been planning this from before she even met him. Anna tried for the side door, but he yanked on the shirt like a leash once more, tearing away the back panel of it entirely. Anna fell to the floor, wailing. He spun the tattered cloth between his hands to make a rope. While she was still crawling, he looped it around her ankles and tied her feet together with ease. He tugged off her shoes, and as she fumbled onto her knees, he ripped off her skirt. The sleeves of her shirt came off next. He kept one in his hand and tossed the other with the discarded pile of clothes on the floor. He tore her underwear off in the same way, leaving her cut and bleeding across her ribs where the underwire came free. He ran a finger along the scratch, revelling in her scream of pain and gathering up the dark red life oozing out of her pale skin on the tip of his finger. He stared at it for a long moment, then she whimpered again, and his passions reignited. He looped the sleeve around her neck for leverage and took her there on the floor of his campervan. She screamed at the beginning but then he just tightened the ligature around her neck until it gurgled away to nothing. Soon the only sounds were the creaking of the suspension, the soft music of the radio and the rhythmic thumping of flesh on flesh. She was dead before he was finished. He took his time cleaning himself up—it wasn't like anyone was going to come along this road in the middle of the night, and even if they did, a parked campervan wasn't going to raise any eyebrows. He tied a knot in the sleeve around her neck and looped it through the knot between her ankles. With a grunt of effort, he could lift Anna's corpse like a piece of luggage. He grinned—that would make things easier.

He followed the road that he had taken with Sarah on their way to their honeymoon, the last time he had felt as satisfied as he did right now. He remembered that there was a nice big patch of empty land by the side of the road on the way to Campbeltown. This late at night, in such an isolated place, he decided to give the girl a little dignity since she had given him such a fun evening. He dug her a shallow grave on a hillside near the village of Skipness, tossed her trussed-up corpse into the two-foot-deep hole and covered it with as much dirt and gravel as he could be bothered to shovel. That was two by strangulation now. Or three if you counted the wee girl from when he was a kid. He kept track of them all in his head as best he could. He knew from his prison buddies that repeating a pattern was the surest way to have the police link up your crimes, so that if they managed to catch you on one they could hammer you for the lot. He wasn't going to make their job any easier. If he could just keep on changing how he did these girls, the police would never be able to connect the dots. They would never be able to pin the crimes on him and he would never have to go back to jail. Angus knew he wasn't the smartest man in the world, but as long as he planned ahead and didn't panic, they were never going to catch him out again.

Digging the grave paid off for Angus; the body of Anna Kenny was not discovered for almost two years. By the time that her body was discovered by a pair of shepherds there was nothing left of it except for her bones, some tiny rotted scraps that might have been the rest of her clothes and the makeshift rope still tied tightly around the bones of her neck and ankles.

Hilda McAuley

The divorce had gone exactly how she wanted and completely ruined her life. Hilda was only a few years off forty and newly single. It was a nightmare. She had gotten both of the kids out of the deal and she had fought for them in the courthouse like they were trying to snatch suckling babes from her arms, but the truth was that the kids were teenagers now and wanted as much to do with their boring old mum as they would have wanted to do with their lecherous old drunk of a father. It had taken her all of two weeks of being divorced to get lonely. To miss the drone of the television in the other room or the snores of a reassuring weight in the bed beside her. She couldn't have kept her husband after all that he had done, but that didn't mean that she had to be alone, did it? There was a whole world full of handsome young men out there and at least one of them wasn't going to turn out to be scum. She was sure of it. All that she had to do was set her sights a little higher. Last time around she had settled for the first man to cross her path, but this time she was going to raise her standards a little. She looked at herself in the bathroom mirror. There were girls jostling her on either side, preening with their hairspray or fidgeting with their makeup to make sure that they were the one to land a cool man tonight. She had at least five years on the oldest of them, and when she looked back at herself after seeing all those pretty young things her dreams all came crashing back down to earth. They looked like they could be on the cover of a magazine. She looked like she could be on an advert for washing powder, if she was lucky.

She was chubby, her hair hung limp about her face like she had just been soaked, her perm was long overdue for a do-over and the longer that she stared at herself the more she heard the voice of her mother echoing back to her from her hen party more than a decade before. 'You'll never do better.'

What a curse to lay on your child, what an insult—she could never do better than that loser? She could never do better than lying awake at night wondering if he was going to come staggering in and climb on top of her like she was part of the furniture? He couldn't do better. She set her jaw. She was the best thing that had ever happened to him and he had squandered it, but there was a room full of men out beyond that swinging door who would be happy to dance with her, and a damn sight more if she would let them. And with rebellion burning in her chest she really thought that she might just let things get out of hand tonight if only to spit in the eye of her mother looking down on her from heaven with disdain.

In a cloud of her own anger, she stormed back out into the Plaza Ballroom and weaved her way through the press of sweating bodies. That one was too short. That one was balding even though he couldn't have been more than twenty years old. That one had his hands on that lassie's thighs and she wouldn't trust him for a second with those shifty eyes of his. One by one she eliminated her potential dancing partners until she reached the bar. There was the usual cavalcade of smells, the fifty different brands of perfume and aftershave that the young ones slathered on all mingling together into a sharp, musky floral mess. The smell of cigarette smoke dominated even that, but beneath it all, there was a weirdly familiar chemical tang that brought Hilda to a halt as she stormed past the bar. It wasn't gin, she was intimately familiar with that, and it wasn't some new drink that they had just cracked open because it was reminding her of her childhood somehow. A smell like her dad in his shed getting ready to spend the weekend fiddling around with the house, something that her husband could never seem to be bothered with even when the cupboard doors were hanging off. That strange familiarity drew her to a sharply dressed man at the bar. He couldn't have been much younger than her, with a full moustache like that. Angus met her gaze with a smile and an appreciative glance up and down that sent shivers running up her back. It had been a while since a man looked at her like that. He bought her a drink and they fell into easy conversation, tossing the odd jibe at the state of the nightlife going downhill every time one of the young ones staggered too close.

It wasn't long until Angus was up and dancing with her, and between the rolling lyrics of Abba's latest hits she could just make out the constant stream of flirtation. The sweet nothings that he was whispering in her ear that hinted at so much more to come. At a night full of adventures, the likes of which she had never seen before when she was shackled to her thug of a husband and trapped in the house by a pair of kids. This man, this Angus, he seemed like a real gentleman. He wasn't trying to get fresh like some of the young lads were doing all around them, though she probably wouldn't have said no if he did. She knew that he wasn't holding back out of a lack of interest—his eyes were raking over her body and he was touching her at every opportunity—so she assumed that it had to be respect, which was an entirely new experience for her.

As the night drew to a close he took her by the arm and led her to the cloakroom. He pressed a whiskery kiss to her cheek and waited as she got her jacket back, then he offered up his arm and they headed out the front door and out onto

Kilmarnock Road. She had a few drinks and she was feeling brave, so she leaned in close and asked him, 'Have you got somewhere we can go?'

The look that he gave her in return could have started a fire. Taking her by the hand, he led her through the dark and fog-shrouded streets until they reached his campervan, hidden away up a side street. She almost laughed out loud. Here he was, all put together and looking handsome, and he drove around in a holiday home on wheels. He must have noticed her expression because he laughed too. 'She might not look like much, but this thing is great. You can go anywhere, anytime and you never have to worry about where you are going to sleep. I drive it every weekend. All over the place. It's a holiday on wheels.'

He pulled the door open with a flourish, and without any better ideas, Hilda rolled her eyes and climbed in.

She made a beeline for the bed and wet her lips in anticipation, but Angus went right through to the driver's seat and gave her a wink. 'Just going to take us somewhere a bit quieter where the police aren't going to come knocking on the windows and disturbing us.'

She laughed. 'Taking me to lover's lane, are you?'

'I might just do that. Come on and sit up here with me. Keep me company.'

They drove for about half an hour, still keeping up the light-hearted banter that had served them both so well back in the dance hall. In the lulls in the conversation, she stared at him. Drinking him in with her eyes. He was younger than her, more vital. Whatever reserves of energy people were born with hadn't run so dry in him yet. When you compared a man like this to her husband, she wondered that it had taken her so long to divorce him. Angus was handsome, and he was smart enough that she didn't feel like she was drawing teeth. He seemed to give exactly the right answer to every question. Even the ones that she didn't ask out loud, like, 'Is this going to happen again?' and 'Could this be the start of something real?'

It had been a long time since she had felt hopeful. Even when she was wrestling through the divorce it had always been lost in the minutiae of court dates and arguments and the ever-present dread about money. Hope was as new an experience to her as respect had been. She felt like she owed a lot to Angus before they had even begun, just for taking her out of the horrible place she had been in her mind. He pulled off the road somewhere up by Port Glasgow and into a quiet little lane where she could see a couple of other parked cars. One of them seemed to be rocking gently from side to side. She blushed despite herself. She knew what she had come here to do but now that she was facing it, it felt sordid.

Angus took her by the hand and led her to the back of the van. She had taken off her jacket already but now her handbag and shoes joined it on the passenger seat. He laid his hands on her and she felt them shaking. He was just as nervous as her! She smiled up at him, finding her courage again, and reached out to undo his belt buckle. He pulled away from her, almost startled. Then he reached down to undo his trousers himself. Feeling daring, Hilda stripped off her own top, exposing herself to a man who wasn't her husband for the first time since teenage fumbles back in school. He reached out a hand and ran it down her shoulder, setting her shuddering all over again. She closed her eyes, savouring the sensation. Which was when he hit her.

The first blow was right in her jaw. It must have stunned her, because the next thing she knew he was on top of her, inside her, and her bra had been torn off. He was crushing her breast in his hand and it was that pain that had dragged her back up from the blissful state of knowing nothing. She drew in a lungful of air to scream and he hit her again, in the eye. She let out a yelp of pain but before she could get a word out he hit her again. And again. His fists fell on her in rhythm with his other movements, battering every bare bit of skin. He had his belt wrapped around one of his hands and he hit her twice as hard on that side when he didn't have to worry about marking his knuckles. Each blow to the head set her ears ringing. Each blow to the body knocked the air from her lungs. He hit her and hit her until she couldn't even feel the pain anymore. All that was left was the thumping of flesh against flesh. Then darkness.

Angus was thrilled—he had never beaten someone to death before. He was tired and aching by the time that he was done but it was a small price to pay for the rush of power he had felt each time his fist collided with that dozy old cow's face. He had finished somewhere in the middle of the beating, but it had felt so good that he just kept on going. He could see the glint of her cheekbone through the bloody wound on her cheek. He could see the bruises already blossoming all over her pallid white flesh. A patina of colour that he had worked into her over the last hour. He had made her look like that. He had made her flesh swell and discolour with his own two hands. He groaned as his knuckles cracked. This sort of thing might have to be saved for special occasions in the future; it took its toll on him too. He was so tired and spent that he didn't even consider the shovel in the closet. He hauled Hilda's body out the side door and tossed her off the side of the road without another thought. Why bother putting any work into hiding her? It wasn't like the police cared. They hadn't even started asking questions about the other ones yet.

The next morning some children were sent to pick brambles across the road from the West Ferry caravan park where they had been spending their October holidays. They found the bloodied and beaten corpse of Hilda in the midst of the bushes, in the centre of a halo of her torn and discarded clothes. Her shoes, handbag and coat were missing. Kept as mementoes of Angus' most exciting kill to date.

The World's End

Gordon and Angus headed out on one of their 'fishing trips' just like every other weekend, and as soon as they rounded the corner they started laughing. It wasn't that they took any great pleasure in lying to Sarah, after all both of them had some measure of affection for her, but it was just so damned easy. Every time they told her the exact same story and even after the truth had filtered back to her about their exploits about town, she still just accepted the lie without a second thought, happy that her husband and brother were getting along so well when all her previous boyfriends had been on the receiving end of Gordon's fists before too long. She was a forgiving soul and if the two men had anything like a functioning human heart between them they would have been riddled with guilt for treating her like a prop in their games.

They'd had good hunting in the nightclubs of Glasgow over the last few months, with Gordon getting off with a different lassie near enough every time Angus was there to work as his wingman. Angus had a charm to him that Gordon had never quite managed to muster. Even when Angus brought him along on decorating jobs you could see him working people over—it was like an art form. The people that he couldn't win over he just navigated around without a flinch. Snubs that would have left Gordon in a rage washed over him like he just didn't care what other people thought of him. Angus was everything that Gordon wanted to be. For his part, Angus appreciated having the extra set of hands around in case he needed to do some heavy lifting, and he liked having someone trustworthy around to tell whatever lies he had fabricated this time. As for the parts that he didn't want any witnesses for at all—people screwed in private. As shameless as Gordon was with his hands all over the poor women in the nightclubs, even he took them someplace secluded before they really started going at it. There had been plenty of nights where he had left Gordon to find his own way home and gone off to do his own business, just as there had been plenty of nights when Gordon had copped off with some girl and left Angus to fend for himself. They might have been friends, in as much as either of them had friends, but they went out with a purpose that they intended on fulfilling and they wouldn't let sentiment get in the way.

As good as Glasgow had been, they were starting to become familiar faces, and while Gordon didn't mind his reputation, Angus didn't need anybody connecting him with the missing girls that everybody seemed to be chatting about. It was less than an hour's drive to the heart of Edinburgh, a place that was familiar enough for the men to feel confident but different enough that they would have fresh pickings. They left early enough that Gordon didn't even complain about the length of time it took them to get through. He just sat in the passenger seat of the campervan, sipping on a tin of beer and working his way through a packet of cigarettes in comfortable silence.

The old town of Edinburgh looked like a different world, like you were going back through time to medieval times. All the concrete of the modern world faded away and the old stone of Arthur's Seat seemed to loom up about you, carved into the vague shapes of buildings, but still fundamentally stone in a way that modern buildings weren't. They got parked a few streets away from the main thoroughfare and walked up the Royal Mile in the late November drizzle. It would be time to start thinking about Christmas soon; some of the tourists and late-night shoppers wandering around them had already gotten the drop on their shopping, nipping into the whiskey shop for a special something or going further afield into the warren of side streets to seek out jewellery shops or other specialists. Angus would have to bring some extra money home if he wanted to keep Sarah and the brat happy. It would mean less time for trips like this, but it would only be a brief interruption to his schedule of worldly pleasures, and if he was smart about it, he would only need to put on a little bit of extra decorating work and a little extra time out in the ice-cream van to cover up all the spare change he was picking up from knocking the crap out of people and stealing their purses, or the envelopes of cash that he got handed every time he delivered one of the more willing girls into the waiting arms of his pornographer buddy. It was hard to strike the balance between the money he was raking in from his criminal enterprises and the legal income that he needed to show to Sarah and the taxman. After years of his comings and goings being ignored by both, he was starting to get lazy about it, and he knew from his time inside that laziness would catch you out as surely as an eyewitness.

There was a longstanding tradition of a pub crawl down the length of the mile, and while both of them already had a little buzz going from the drive over from Glasgow, it was going to need topping off pretty promptly if they wanted to keep on partying all night. They made it to the top of the long slope and looked down. It was so steep that you could trip up and roll all the way to the old gates of the city if you were unlucky enough. Angus pretended to shove Gordon, drawing a cackle from the younger man, before the two of them ducked into the first of many bars that they were going to be visiting that evening. This high up the hill they didn't even bother to look at the women, although there were already a few of them out and about. There were work nights out and the usual crop of day drinkers, but none of them were ready to go off for a tumble so early in the evening. There was a reason they had parked at the foot of the hill. It was like the stupid animal documentaries that Sarah put on for the kid because they were 'educational'. Angus wasn't going to go flinging himself into the midst of all the healthy specimens that could make a run for it, he would wait to pick off the weak stragglers at the end of the night. The ones who were too drunk or too young to know better.

It was a waiting game, but it was one that the men were more than familiar with. They kept themselves topped off with drinks and engaged in as much inane conversation as they could stomach. They spent enough time with each other that the silence was easy, but men sitting in silence drew attention, so they had to keep up the chatter. Sports usually handled most of the conversational heavy lifting, along with some shared acquaintances and stories about the family. When there was a long enough lull in the conversation, they got up and moved on to the next bar where they would start the cycle all over again. By the third pub, they had started to do a little bit of flirting, just to warm up. By the fourth, Angus was starting to put a little effort in, passing the friends of his chosen girls along to Gordon almost as an afterthought. If one of these girls had taken him up on his sly glances, then he probably wouldn't have said no. It wasn't the plan, but who gave a damn about a plan when the girl was right there?

Angus did his best to keep himself on the plateau where he was drunk enough that everything was fun but not so drunk that he slurred his words. Finding the balance over the course of an hour was easy enough but minute to minute there were some hiccoughs, which he blamed for his failure to get one of the girls on the hook. He skipped the next round of drinks and let the cold harsh edges of sobriety creep back into the periphery of his vision. All the passions that the booze damped down came back to torment him in moments like this, when his blood was up and there was no ready and willing outlet for his fury. He grabbed Gordon by the back of his collar and pulled him out of the conversation he had been inveigling himself into. He didn't let his anger or disappointment show on his face, but the empty expression, the mask of humanity was almost worse for Gordon to look at. At least when Angus was angry an ending was in sight. When he was unhappy, it was completely out of Gordon's control.

Gordon knew his brother-in-law had a troubled past, and he liked to imagine that some dark event in his history was what kept bringing misery back around on him rather than it just being some inherent flaw in his makeup. Sarah knew what

Angus had done in the past, he was sure of that, but his sister was a good person and she was still happily married to the man, so it had to have been something that happened to Angus rather than something that he had done himself. That was the only thing that made sense to Gordon, even if it made him uncomfortable to think of Angus as anything less than he was right now: the pinnacle of everything a man might want to be.

Out in the street, the rain had finally petered to a halt and that seemed to be enough to bring Angus back up from his sudden pit of depression. He slipped a smile back onto his face and flung an arm around Gordon's shoulders. It was going to be a good night, Angus could feel it in his bones. He knew it was going to be a good night because he was going to get exactly what he wanted. He always got what he wanted. He was entitled to satisfaction, just the same as every one of the other morons strolling down this street in the dark. They might find their satisfaction a bit easier, but it was the same thing and it wasn't fair that he had to work so much harder than them before he could feel happy. Gordon just needed a couple of pints and a girl to lay hands on and he was content for the week. Wasn't Angus allowed the same? He bumped Gordon with his shoulder, sending him staggering into the gutter with a yelp and a laugh. The two of them made their way down to the last pub of the night, the last one on the mile; The World's End.

Inside, it was standing room only. The owners understood that volume drove their business and they were selling pints and bottom shelf liquor for only a pound. With two hundred bodies crammed into that tiny pub from dinner time onwards, they could afford to be generous. Angus let himself get drunker here, get sloppier than he would have dared earlier in the evening. By this time of night, it was expected, and it was easier to endure the constant bumping and elbows with a fine alcoholic haze over the whole thing. He spotted more than a few good prospects in the crowd, girls who were young enough or drunk enough to be viable entertainment for the rest of the night. He couldn't say that he cared whether or not they were pretty, although it was always a bonus. The pretty ones started off more defensive though, and he wasn't sure that he was in the mood for the thrill of the hunt tonight. Sometimes he just wanted simple satisfaction. Then the crowd parted, and he saw the two girls huddled around a tiny table at the back wall. Young, isolated and pretty enough that Gordon would be pleased. Angus pressed his way through the crowd and the wall of noise until he was close enough to give them his patented grin. 'There aren't many tables about, do you girls mind if we share?'

The prey looked nervous and sheepish, they weren't sure what this was, whether it was a come on or some other sort of trick. That was good. He wanted them off balance. He wanted them confused. They couldn't fend him off if they didn't know what he was after. Angus gestured down at his work clothes. 'No funny business girls, I've just been on my feet all day. I'll get the next round in, shall I? What are you having?'

This was the only moment of real risk, leaving the slightly tipsy Gordon to watch over them and drive away any competition while he got the drinks. Gordon was reliable enough, but he hadn't perfected his patter the way that Angus had. He couldn't talk a girl who said no around to a yes, or a girl who said yes around to more. The best you could hope for with Gordon was that he could keep things neutral. He made it back to the table without much incident and discovered the three of them chatting away like old friends. Good work Gordon, he had earned a treat tonight. Angus slipped into the conversation like a scalpel, so sharp you didn't even notice him cutting in. They went through all the usual topics that the men had heard a dozen times with the other women in the other bars—practice really did make perfect. The girls were laughing and smiling much more often than they weren't, and the few missteps got covered with the next joke so quickly that the inebriated teenagers didn't even have a chance to notice them. During one of their loudest outburst of giggles, Angus leaned in close and hissed in Gordon's ear, 'Which one do you want?'

Gordon shrugged. 'Both look good to me, mate.'

Angus grinned. 'You want both? You want to swap about?'

Gordon looked intrigued. 'You think they'd go for that, do you?'

Angus laughed, blending back into the girls' conversation. 'You think it is up to them?'

The last call bell rang not long after, but the girls showed no signs of being tired. They got a last drink in and when Gordon started fumbling towards inviting the girls somewhere else, Angus cut him off with another inane story. The time wasn't right yet, they had to strike in the moment when the girls were at their most vulnerable, not when they were safe and warm in the back of a pub filled with friends. The crowd started to thin, and the barman kept glancing back at their table, which they took as a sign that it was time to move along. Still, Angus held back, and Gordon followed his lead. The girls were weaving and stumbling on the way to the door and Angus could feel the moment of opportunity approaching—one would stumble, and he would catch her and imply that they weren't safe to get home alone. He could see it all lining up in his mind right now. As one of the girls—he never bothered to learn names—stepped out of the front door of the World's End, the opportunity arose. She started to fall but even before Angus started to dash forward to catch her an alarm bell started ringing in the back of his mind and he turned away, as if lost in conversation with one of the other patrons. A policeman had stepped up and caught the girl, less than six feet from where Angus was standing. He could hear his blood roaring in his ears. He hadn't been seen. He definitely hadn't been recognised because there was no roar and outcry. He was still invisible. He was still safe. After the policeman had turned away he saw Gordon swoop in to take the girl by the arm and share a laugh with her. That was good. That was what Angus should have done if he hadn't been so shaken by the sight of that uniform.

Angus offered his arm to the other girl like a gentleman and led her out into the street. He gave them a moment for the cold and the dark to really sink into their skin, for them to realise what they would be stepping off into all alone, then he asked. 'Hey, we're heading off to a party next. You two are coming, right?'

One of them started to shake her head but the other one, now snuggled in under Gordon's arm answered for them both. 'Of course. It's the weekend, isn't it?'

Angus smiled again, so wide that his cheeks ached, then he led them off into the dark.

Inside the campervan they kept the party going. Passing around cans of lager and taking ticklish sips from tiny bottles of BabyCham as the girls cackled and mouthed back to each other, 'Love the BabyCham', as if they were in the advert from the cinema. Angus said that they were heading to a house out in suburbia and without missing a beat Gordon started furnishing the girls with details about the imaginary party. Gordon was doing such a good job of keeping the girls entertained that they didn't even notice that they had left the city entirely. Angus was starting to consider bringing the young lad along on every single 'fishing trip' if he continued to be this useful. Right out in the middle of the pitch black nowhere, Angus pulled the van over between the hedgerows and turned off the engine. The girls were still mid giggle, but one of them managed to ask, 'Are we finally at the party?'

Angus grinned and unbuckled his belt. 'We brought all the party you're going to need with us, darling. Now, which one of you lovely ladies wants to go first?'

They looked at each other, still giggling away. The sound of their mockery was like nails being hammered directly into Angus' brain. 'I said which one of you wants to be fucked first?'

Gordon was looking at Angus with something like horror on his face. He had never seen his brother-in-law behaving like this before and he wasn't sure if the disgust churning in his gut was enough to overcome the raw embarrassment or the treacherous spark of excitement inside him. The girls looked at him for confirmation that this was just a joke, and he made his decision. His eyebrows drew down and he growled, 'Him or me. Which one do you want first?'

One of the girls made a break for the door but Angus was already there, grabbing her by the hair and tossing her onto the floor like she was nothing. The other one was still sitting paralysed beside Gordon, so he took a hold of her wrist in case she tried anything stupid. Angus drew some cord out of his pocket. It must have been there all night. All day that they had been together, he had that rope in his pocket and he was planning this. That knowledge was like electricity on Gordon's skin. This wasn't a night gone wrong, this was Angus' plan going perfectly right. He was part of the plan. He tightened his grip on the girl's wrist as Angus tied up the one who had tried to escape. With a smirk, Angus tossed him what was left of the rope. He wet his lips. 'Do her.'

Then he picked his girl up by the hair and dragged her across to the bed as she screamed. There was a sound of ripping cloth from behind them and Gordon tried to concentrate on what he was doing, his numb fingers fumbling the knots that Angus had made look so easy a moment ago. The girl was sobbing now, straining to see what was happening to her friend, as if she wasn't about to experience it first-hand. Gordon didn't have the same fury as Angus. When he had the girl tied up he carefully unzipped and unbuttoned her clothes, tugging them up and down without being able to remove them completely. Eventually, he gave up and just climbed on top of her.

The screaming was punctuated by other sounds now. There was a steady percussion of flesh and bone colliding, but some of it was Angus' fists pummelling his girl every time she made a sound. When she stopped screaming, he hammered into her harder until she made a noise again to excuse the next round of violence. By the time he was done with her, the pretty young girl that they had met in the World's End was fading behind the deep red of blossoming bruises. Drool, tears and snot were pouring down her face. Angus had stuffed her torn panties into her mouth, but it did little to silence the deep guttural moaning.

When it was Gordon's turn he couldn't even look at her. He just stared down at her chest as he mechanically moved against her. The girl he had taken first was shrieking now from whatever Angus was doing to her and Gordon was losing his rhythm. Intrusive thoughts were creeping in. How were they going to keep these girls quiet when they were done? There was no way that they wouldn't recognise mugshots. There was no way that they weren't going to go running to the police. He had slowed in his movements and the girl beneath him was letting out a low steady moan, more animal than human. She was twisted around, trying not to look at Gordon as he raped her, but she had ended up watching Angus as he worked over her friend instead. The screams from Angus' side turned to gurgles, and Gordon was forced to look over too.

Angus was choking the girl with another length of cord. He was inside her and he was choking her to death. Gordon's stomach turned but he kept thrusting. The girl beneath him let out a wail, so he hammered into her harder and faster, trying to forget what was happening beside him. Trying to forget what he was an accomplice to. Just as he was about to finish he leaned in close to her ruined face and barked out.

'See what is happening to her? He is going to do you next. You are next.'

She started sobbing, and that was all Gordon needed.

Angus dragged the dead girl out of the van and off into a field, still naked from the waist down and shivering in the cold night's air. Gordon looked from him to the girl still breathing in the campervan and he had a brief wild moment when he thought about letting her go. Surely, she wouldn't klipe on him. Not when he had just saved her life from Angus? He pushed the thought away as he scrambled back into his clothes. Angus wouldn't let her live after what she had seen, and he couldn't let Gordon live either if he thought that there was even a chance that he might betray him. Gordon had to prove that he was loyal. That he could be trusted with this last secret part of Angus that he had never seen before and never planned to see again. Angus found his trousers when he got back into the campervan but as he pulled them up he paused to wiggle his backside at Gordon, who choked on his own laughter. The girl didn't say anything. She was just lying there now, beaten bloody and trying to hide from the world outside by retreating into her own mind. It wouldn't help.

Angus nodded at her. 'We'll take that one someplace else. That way they might find one and not the other, should just be a quick drive.'

Gordon nodded nervously then joined Angus in the front seats. 'You know Angus, I've never done anything like this before...'

Angus chuckled, 'Aye, I could tell. Don't worry. I'm not going to make you finish her off. I'm not a complete bastard. I can see you're shaken.'

Gordon let out another wheezing laugh. 'I'm just not used to this sort of thing. You know. Like, I appreciate everything you've done for me, and I appreciate getting a turn on the two lassies last night but...'

'You pussying out on me? Is that it? Is it all getting a bit too scary?'

'Aye. That's right. I didn't sign up to kill any lassies. Just to have a good time.'

Angus snorted. 'That was a good time. Are you kidding? You're trying to tell me that wasn't the most fun you've ever had?'

'That is exactly what I am trying to tell you.'

Angus fell silent for a moment as he pulled out onto the main road, then he shrugged his shoulders. 'Alright then. I'm not going to make you do something you don't want to.'

'And I'll not say anything about this to anybody,' Gordon added. Angus shook his head. 'Of course you won't you silly bastard. You are the accomplice to the murder of two young lassies. They'd have you in the nick for the rest of your life if you were daft enough to say anything to anybody. I know you,

Gordie, you might not be the smartest lad in the world but you're not that stupid.'

Gordon fell back into silence. The only sound was the van's engine and the sniffing sobs from in the back. Angus nodded in that direction. 'We'll be driving for a bit if you want another go on her. She isn't as pretty as she used to be but I'm sure you could find something to do with yourself.'

Gordon suppressed a shudder. 'I'm fine thanks. Not much face left for kissing is there? You really did a number on her.'

Angus smirked. 'I told her not to scream. Isn't my fault she wouldn't do as she was told.'

When they arrived at the next field it was closer to dawn than to midnight and the hard day's drinking and exercise were starting to take its toll. Angus choked the life out of the girl with his bare hands as she let out little croaks. But he was too tired to really squeeze, so he just put all of his weight on her instead. Her windpipe collapsed under the pressure, but she didn't pass out the way she would have if he had been squeezing her the way he was meant to. The one eye that wasn't completely sealed in with swelling bulged out of her head as she tried to gasp for air and she writhed about. Even in these final moments, she was still trying to save herself. Trying to escape. Before another minute had passed, she flopped down, limp. Angus watched her carefully for a few minutes more, then when he was certain that she was dead, he had Gordon take her ankles and between the two of them they hoisted her up and tossed her into the field. Angus spat in the ditch and lit a cigarette, looking up at the stars stretching out above them. 'You never see them in the city, do you?'

Gordon looked up and tried to pretend that it was just the pricking cold making his eyes water. 'No, you never do.'

Angus was grinning, but he still hadn't quite been sated. Two at once wasn't doing the trick, and the added stress of managing Gordon was more trouble than it was worth. He needed something new to keep the fire burning. He needed change. He blinked the stars out of his eyes and gave Gordon a pat on the shoulder. The boy was shivering but Angus couldn't bring himself to care, what a wasted opportunity Gordon had turned out to be. They clambered back into the van and Angus sighed. At least now he was guaranteed the boy's loyalty. There was no lie too ridiculous for Gordon to repeat after what he had seen and done tonight. Angus had him by the balls for the rest of his life. Accomplice to murder. Rape. They were the chains that he could use to bind Gordon for the rest of time. The boy had only a few limited uses, but now there didn't need to be any fair trade. He didn't have to furnish the boy with dancing partners and booze in exchange for his silence now. All that he had to do was give him his marching orders. Not the worst outcome that tonight could have had, but not as good as a full-time subservient partner could have been.

Agnes Cooney

Being a nurse meant being on your feet all day, every day, and nobody knew that better than Agnes Cooney. That meant that the few precious days she wasn't working, she liked to have a nice long lie in her bed and a good portion of the day sitting on her backside. Hiking all over the city looking for a new place to live, even in the company as pleasant as her best friend Gina, was not her idea of a good time. She could tell that Gina was feeling equally cheerful after they had been to see the third flat up three flights of tenement stairs. They had taken the morning to themselves and met at midday with the property agent. They had both had enough by dinnertime. Gina looked like she was ready to drop, and Agnes didn't feel much better. The south side of Glasgow had been Agnes' home for a good few years now while she worked in the children's ward, and while she wouldn't claim to know it like the back of her hand, she knew it well enough to find her way through the warrens of streets to find Westmoreland Street and the Clada Social Club, where they could sit down and have a quiet drink for the rest of the night without threats of dancing or more walking. A couple of drinks turned into a couple more and the night stretched on and on until midnight closing arrived and Agnes realised with a groan that she had to be up again in the morning for her shift. She gave Gina a hug goodbye and headed out the door to look for a taxi, waving her arms at traffic as she made her way along the street in the hope of one spotting her before she finally found the taxi rank. It didn't take long for a campervan to swing up to the pavement beside her and for the passenger door to pop open. Angus gave Agnes a big smile, 'You need a lift home, hen?'

In her addled state, she took his van for a taxi and his catcall as an invitation. He helped haul her up into the seat beside him and then he drove off. Before long she dozed off in the warmth and the gentle rocking. Angus had never had such easy pickings. He had barely driven fifty feet away from the door of the tenement in Glasgow where he had been staying recently before a fresh victim was proudly presenting itself on the side of the road. It was good timing. He had been itching to try something new ever since those daft wee girls from Edinburgh had turned out to be such a disappointment.

The drive out to Lanarkshire was almost completely peaceful. Angus found himself almost bubbling over with energy that had no outlet. Normally he would be smoothing things over, laying on lie after lie to keep the girl complacent, but tonight everything had just fallen into his lap. There had been no work. There had been no hunt. It was like the universe just wanted to give him this moment of release without making him work for it. He wasn't sure that he liked it. At least it gave him some time to think, some time to plan ahead. He knew that he wanted to try something new and this was the perfect opportunity to stretch his creativity. He caught himself drumming his fingers on the steering wheel and frowned. There would be plenty of time for action soon.

When they arrived somewhere suitably devoid of human life, he hauled the girl back through to the bed in the back, but she barely stirred from her stupor. Angus briefly wondered if the girl had been drugged, if some other bastard had been stalking her all night and doing all of his legwork for him, but she came around just fine when he started to tear her clothes off. Once he had her completely naked he twisted her clothes into something like ropes and bound her. It wouldn't do for the police to find the same twine on too many corpses. Connections got you caught. Fear had driven all of the sleepy drunkenness from her body in a wash of adrenaline. Her eyes weren't just open, they were bulging wide and white as he pushed inside her with his hand clamped tight over her mouth. He hammered away at her until he drew blood, but it still wasn't doing anything for him. He slipped his hand down to squeeze her neck, and while it did make other parts of her flex and tremor in interesting ways, it still wasn't enough. Nothing was ever enough to sate this hunger. Nothing could scratch this itch. He needed more.

He didn't remember picking up the knife, he certainly didn't remember hiding it back here under the pillow to begin with. Perhaps it was more serendipity. Maybe she was meant to end up here. Maybe he was meant to do this. That would explain why he wanted to so badly. He was fulfilling his purpose in all of this. He traced the blade down between her breasts, drawing a red line on her pale skin and drawing a frantic panting from her panty-gagged mouth. That seemed to work. He started moving again, the knife's tip bouncing with each thrust, just barely brushing her skin. Just letting her feel the sharpness without ever going deeper. Soon he was panting right back, and she was letting out high pitched shrieks that sent sparks of pleasure shooting up his spine. It was almost enough. He was so close to his satisfaction that he could already taste the coppery flavour on his lips. He slammed the knife down into her stomach and he felt like the life was being torn out of him in each gasping breath. With the next thrust of the knife, his eyes rolled up into his head and he let out a guttural roar. He had never felt pleasure like this, he had never been so powerful as when that knife passed so easily through her skin to dig into the hidden things down below. Again and again, he stabbed into her. With each one, his joy grew greater and more all-encompassing until in the end, he could feel nothing but sweet release and delight.

When he came back down it was like the only time he had used the diving board at the local pool. He went from the blissful joy of flying to a sudden horrible impact, then nothing more than the sensation of being soaking wet. When he looked down, all that he could see was red. His clothes, the bed, everything was soaked in blood. Thick and dripping with it. Gore was trickling down to puddle about his feet, running in rivulets down his legs from the raw mess that he had made out of this girl's body. He tried to count the number of stab wounds but kept losing count about twenty. His head was pounding like he had a hangover from a three-day bender. He had to remember to breathe as he tried to pull his mind back together.

He looked down at the gruesome remains of his evening's pleasure and he said, 'Bollocks.' He needed to clean this up. He needed to get rid of the body and wash himself. He would need to scrub out the whole campervan. He would probably have to replace the whole mattress. He doubted it could be saved, even if the quilt had soaked up most of the outpouring of his passion. The whole campervan reeked like a slaughterhouse, the sharp iron tinge of blood undercut by the faint hint of offal and the putrid tang of ruptured bowels. He had done this. He had made a woman into nothing more than a heap of meat. He tried to scoop up the blood that was pouring down onto the floor and slop it back up onto the bed, but he gave up and collapsed in a fit of laughter. Maybe hungover wasn't the right word for it. He was still drunk on all of that power. Aftershocks were still rippling through his body. Between the moments of altered consciousness, his mind slowly fell back into its old mechanical patterns, calculating his best odds. He would toss the corpse, find one of his regular fishing spots to wash up and burn whatever couldn't be salvaged from the back of the van. She was slippery to the touch and he had to hook his fingers into wounds and crevices to get a grip on her at all, so instead of an arduous hike, he just tossed her right out of the side door of the van without even bothering to hide her from plain sight. What did it matter if the police found her, there was nothing connecting him to her. No witnesses. No motive. No connection to his other killings. Nothing. He was going to get away with murder, forever.

Mary Gallacher

Fixing up the mess he had made in the campervan wasn't going to be quick or cheap, and having it out of action meant that Angus had lost one of the main weapons in his arsenal. Life had gone in an instant from being a pleasure cruise to a hard grind once again. He needed money and he needed release. His fairly lucrative business supplying nude models to Eddie Cotogno was starting to dry up, with the old man getting more and more reluctant to hand over cash for the few girls that Angus was delivering. Without the campervan, transporting the girls to Eddie was getting too complicated, and even if he did manage to snare a girl, in his current agitated state he would be as likely to take her for himself as sell her along. Acting out like that was a good way to get caught and Angus had no intention of ever going back to jail. Not when the world was full of such sweet and easily plucked fruit.

He had to control himself, and the easiest way to do that was to keep himself out of situations where he might be tempted.

His 'fishing trips' with Gordon had wound down over the last few weeks, ending entirely when the campervan was put out of action. Gordon got the impression that he had failed some sort of test, and that Angus didn't consider him cool anymore, but he was so scared of the man it was almost a relief to get away from him. He didn't let any of this slip to Sarah of course, he just said that the cold weather had made fishing into a chore and went on lavishing his usual praise on her husband.

Without the cash from Cotogno, and with the drudgery of regular working life looking as appealing as it ever had, Angus fell back on his old favourite money maker as a way to vent some of his violent impulses while also moving towards his goal: muggings. He committed a string of brutal attacks around the estates of Glasgow, never even giving people the chance to hand over their cash before stabbing them or beating them unconscious. He soon lost count of how many of these vicious attacks he had committed, and despite his business interests earning little-to-no money over the last few years, Angus always had enough money for a new car, a deposit on a new house or to cover his skyrocketing bar tabs. Before long he had the money to refurbish his campervan, but he went on mugging while he waited for the repairs to be completed as a means to alleviate the other, internal, pressures.

Mary Gallacher was just 17 years old when she left her family home in Glasgow to go and visit a pair of friends a few streets over. She didn't bother with a coat despite the chill because she was only going to be outside for a few minutes, taking a shortcut over to Avonspark Street. She had no way of knowing what was lying in wait for her in the waste-ground between the streets of Springburn. Angus had been out hunting fruitlessly for most of the early evening. The only other people he had seen risking this well-tread shortcut had been in groups, or homeless, and while there might have been some fun to be had stabbing some useless old codger, there was no way they were going to have any money, and mugging was ostensibly still what he was doing. If he was out here just for the fun of hurting people then that would make him sick and twisted, but robbing people was normal, even if it did feel good. He had met plenty of perverts in prison, people who had wires crossed and did sick things because it got their motors running. He wasn't like that. He wasn't willing to be one of them. He did what he had to do to get what he wanted but what he wanted was the same perfectly normal thing that every other man wanted. He was sure of that.

He forgot all of that justification almost instantly the moment that Mary came into sight. He felt stirrings in his gut, and his hand tightened around the hilt of the knife hidden in his pocket. She might not have any money, but she had something that he needed even more. It didn't matter that there was nowhere to go. It didn't matter that the sun had only just dipped below the horizon. He wanted her, and he was going to have her. He followed her across the waste-ground, stalking her like a wild animal following its prey, stepping softly and keeping quiet until she was close enough to touch. At the last moment, when they were almost touching, he pulled out the knife and pressed it against her back with a growl. She let out a yelp of surprise before he could clamp his hand over her mouth. He leaned in so close that his breath was tickling across her cheek. 'Make another noise and you are dead. Do what I say, and you get to walk away alive. Got it?'

She froze for a long moment, then nodded, pressing against his grip with each movement. Angus grinned. 'Start walking. That way.'

He led her further out into the empty space where construction was yet to begin. A desolate land of abandoned furniture, half-stolen building supplies and toppled fences. When he felt sure that they were far enough out, he twisted her around and pushed her down to the ground. In the dim light, he loomed over her like an obelisk, barking orders. 'Strip.'

Mary started to cry but he took a step closer, letting the moonlight shimmer off the blade of his knife. 'Take off your kit or you're never going home.'

Mary fell into quiet sobs, her shoulders shuddering as she slowly pulled up her top. Angus' grin threatened to take the top off his head. Her pale skin looked ghostly in the moonlight. Her face was so deep in shadows that it looked like a skull. He grabbed her by the hair and tilted her head back, a brief spike of anxiety washing away when the light played over her features. Tears were streaming down her cheeks in a pale shimmer. He yanked the straps of her bra off her arms and dragged it painfully down around her waist as she tried desperately not to scream.

'Take off the trousers.'

She managed to splutter, 'Why?'

'Why do you think? Take them off or I'll cut them off.'

With shaking fingers, she unbuttoned them and pushed them down. He grabbed one of the legs and yanked as hard as he could, but it just caused Mary to topple over. He tugged on them again and again, dragging her bare back across the rough ground and drawing more screams from her. He got them off and dropped down on top of her, crushing her into the stony ground and driving the air out of her lungs.

She slapped him, almost accidentally, as she flailed around and for a moment he froze. She hit him again as he fumbled with her underwear, then she hooked her fingers into claws and raked them across his face as he pushed inside her. It was his turn to scream. One of her nails scraped over his eye and he tried to jerk away. Now that he was on top of her, now that the worst was already happening, all her fear seemed to have left her. She started to scream at the top of her lungs, she beat him around the head with her fists as he tried to rape her.

'Stop it. Stop it. Stop it. You're ruining everything,' he growled at her, but she couldn't hear him over her own hoarse shrieking. She scraped her nails down his neck, drawing blood, and that was enough. His fury erupted. He was only allowed one thing in this world, one moment of satisfaction and she was ruining it. Why couldn't she just do what she was meant to do? Why wouldn't she just submit?

She bellowed right in his ear, 'Help! Help me!'

Fear blossomed up inside of Angus, strangling his lust and anger before they could even truly form. She was being too loud. She was going to draw attention. He should never have done this out here. He should have just waited until it was safe. Until he had somewhere safe to take her. This was stupid. He was going to get caught. He was going to go back to jail.

He started to wilt, and that just gave Mary more confidence. She dug her fingers into his eye, she bit his hand when he tried to muffle her screaming and every little interruption made it more difficult for him to keep going. He fell back off of her and felt something soft under his hand instead of the mud and grit he expected. Her trousers. He lunged forward again, with his new garotte in hand. He wrapped the leg of the trousers around her throat and as she gurgled and choked he felt his strength and vigour returning. He thrust down into her like he was trying to drive her under the earth. Like he was trying to bury her alive. He could hear himself think again. He could hear his own laboured and ragged breathing. Now that silence had fallen again it was as though his sense of hearing had become hyperacute. He was straining to hear anything that might be going on. Straining for the first sign of danger. He was still distracted. He still couldn't enjoy himself. She had ruined it. He hammered into her harder. Her dragged the trouser leg tighter around her throat, but no matter how much he choked the life out of her she still pushed against him. She still made gurgling sounds that sounded deafening in his ears. It wasn't enough. He still wasn't in control. He fumbled around on the ground beside her until his fingers brushed over the sharp edge of his knife. He dragged it over her throat and waited for the usual bliss to wash over him, but it never came.

Blood soaked into the trouser leg but somehow, she was still moving. Still making the wet gargling sounds that were echoing out across the barren land and back from the sides of the abandoned, half-made buildings scattered all around them. Her eyes were still open. She was still glowering at him, even as her hot blood spurted out all over his hands. She was still alive. He could see her hands balling into his fists. She was going to hit him again. He hated her. He hated every inch of her. He regretted the moment he had laid eyes on her. She had ruined everything. He cut into her neck again, deeper this time. Still she writhed beneath him. He cut again and again. Finally, he dragged himself up her body and put his full weight behind the blade. He cut so deeply that the knife scraped over bone and finally she stopped fighting him. He let out a shuddering breath and felt all the strength leaving his body. He collapsed on top of the rapidly cooling corpse and sobbed. Relief washed over him, but not release. She had stolen that from him. She had made him kill her for nothing. He forced himself to get up and fasten up his clothes, but that was all that he had the energy for. She had ruined everything. All of the confidence. All of the power that he had been gathering around himself since he left prison had been stripped away. He felt like the terrified child that he had been back when he first started touching little girls. He could feel all the eyes of the world on him. Seeing him for what he was. Seeing the terrible things that he had done. He staggered away from Mary's corpse without a backward glance. He broke into a stumbling run as soon as he could draw a breath. She had ruined everything.

Living in Fear

Even with the campervan back in action and his wife's suspicions fading away to almost nothing, Angus still couldn't bring himself to abduct another woman. He was a coward at heart, and while he had managed to convince both himself and those around him that he was well adjusted and confident, those things could not be further from the truth. Even his muggings, the only outlet that he had for all of his aggressive sexual energies, began to drop in number as he lost his confidence. Eventually, he resorted to the same route that weak and cowardly men have throughout history when they needed to feel powerful again. He bought a handgun.

While gun ownership was still legal in Scotland after the Firearms Act of 1968, it was restricted to those who had a license to own a weapon—generally, rural workers who would need the weapon for their work or members of fairly elite gun clubs. Angus wasn't a farmer, he didn't go to a rifle club, and if you had asked him about clay pigeons he probably would have assumed it was slang for some sort of drug. He purchased his gun from a man in a pub, entirely illegally, and stored it in the campervan, as a totem of strength more than as an actual tool—he never actually pointed it at another person as long as he owned it.

Without the confidence to abduct and murder women, Angus was becoming more and more withdrawn and miserable. His already paper-thin façade of civility to his neighbours began to fray and his relationship with his wife suffered to the point where he was spending half of his time living with his sickly brother rather than with his family. He knew that if he didn't do something soon, he was going to have a dangerous outburst that would likely land him back in prison.

He returned to doing what he knew best. He would travel around the housing estates, using his ice-cream van as cover, and lure young girls into the closes of tenements where he would brutally rape them. He used a variety of methods and lies to snare the girls, being careful not to link anything back to his ice cream selling business. A favourite trick was to claim he had lost his dog and needed the girl to check in the close for it while he searched the street. He even carried a leash to accentuate the lie. Every week he would go out hunting and almost as often, he would find a young girl between the ages of six and fourteen, about the same age as his own son, and have his way with her. Before long, even he lost count of how many girls he had molested and raped. When questioned about it by the police, decades later, he said that it could have been fifty or five hundred.

One of the more unusual reports about the way he was hunting his victims didn't come until decades later when his face was recognised in a newspaper by someone who had been a little girl at the time. She claimed that Angus had approached her in his car outside the school, trying to convince her to get inside. Obviously, Angus was known to the police by this point in his life, and there were a great many people about, so he was forced to adopt a disguise. According to this witness, Angus was wearing a sundress and had caked makeup on over his usual dark stubble to try and pass himself off as a woman. The girl at the time had been too mesmerized by the strange juxtaposition of what was obviously a man speaking in a falsetto voice to get the idea that he could be dangerous in any way. She almost got into the car with him out of pure curiosity before her mother spotted her and Angus sped away. If this cross-dressing was normal for Angus, it might explain what he had been doing with all of the clothing that he had stolen from his victims as trophies through the years, but in all likelihood this story is just one of the many folk tales that spread out in the wake of Angus' capture and the public interest in the case.

It became commonplace for Angus, and with time he was able to get his compulsions back under control and draw his family back together once again. His family moved in with Maimie in a semi-detached house in Glasgow, along with his sister's daughter Heather. Maimie was now in her 70s and her health was beginning to deteriorate to the point that she needed almost daily assistance.

The rapes and molestations were all being reported to the police, but without any evidence to draw the cases together, they had no reason to suspect that they were all the actions of a single sick man. It was enough to keep Angus behaving like a sane man on normal days, but when he was put under pressure, his true nature would come out.

Eddie Cotogno had been a steady source of income over the years, and now with his other hobbies lapsed, Angus began to spend more time with the old man and learning about photography. Angus' interest extended beyond simply snapping pictures. Like Eddie, he wanted to be able to develop any photographs that he took without having to worry about the curious eyes of the local pharmacist. The old man had taken the time to teach him how to develop black and white pictures quite early in their partnership, but with more free time, Angus was now pushing him to teach him how to develop colour. Eddie had more important things to do, so he kept fobbing the man off with excuses. He had no idea that Angus had become a ticking time bomb without the steady release that abducting and murdering women had granted him.

Angus still did his best to introduce as many girls to Eddie as possible, and to take as many pictures as he could. Without so many of them being consumed by his own appetites the volume of women that he presented to the pornographer began to climb once more, as did the variety of 'special projects' he was able to complete for his partner in crime. Eddie was pleased, but he also wanted to teach the younger man a lesson about respect, so he began to pay less for each girl than he had before the slump and gave Angus a smaller cut from the payments that they were receiving in exchange for their more exotic pictures. Angus noticed immediately, but he didn't confront Eddie, as he still hoped to draw the secret of colour photo development out of him, presumably so that he could cut the old man out of the deal altogether. Angus was trying to keep him sweet, while Eddie was trying to antagonise the young man into saying something so that he could slap him down for abandoning him during the long dry spell.

This went on for months until eventually, Angus' temper got the better of him. The argument started with yet another excuse from Eddie about why he didn't have the time to teach someone as simple as Angus about the complex chemical procedures required to develop colour pictures, but soon it escalated into a screaming match about the reduced payments and every other slight that Angus thought that the old man had sent his way. Eddie still did not know who he was dealing with. So, he snapped back at Angus without a second thought, tearing into him about the low quality and quantity of 'raw materials' he was providing and excusing his reduced payments as a result of those shortcomings. He finally got to pour out all of his anger about the long months when Angus had abandoned him, leaving him with no models and no hope of fulfilling his special orders. Angus had no answer for this torrent of abuse, so he resorted to his fists. Eddie was nearly as old as Angus' frail old mother and he suffered from numerous health complaints of his own. It was no surprise that he couldn't stop Angus as the man beat him to the ground, seized Eddie's camera and began clubbing him to death with it.

Even when Eddie was dead and twitching on the floor, it still wasn't enough for Angus. He tore through the house, gathering up all of the old man's filthy pictures and scattering them all around his corpse for the whole world to find. It was the greatest punishment that Angus could think of. To make the whole world see what Eddie had been doing. To shame him, the way that Angus had been shamed in the courtroom. It only took a few minutes for Angus to calm down and realise how stupid he was being. He couldn't leave the corpse just lying in the middle of the living room, waiting to be found and to whisper all its secrets to the forensics team that would investigate the murder. He had to cover it up. Luckily, in the black room that occupied most of the ground floor, there were a multitude of hazardous—and highly flammable—chemicals that he could use.

Angus was not accustomed to starting fires—he was a city boy, through and through, and in his experience fire was something that existed only within the safe confines of a gas fireplace or an oven. He was not prepared for how quickly Eddie and the house would go up in flames and he had to run to escape unburnt. He fled the scene even as the distant sound of fire engines began to wail their way across Dumbarton.

Once again, anything resembling justice seemed to have passed Angus by. The police investigation into the death of Eddie Cotogno, a man that many on the force had secretly wanted out of the picture for a very long time, came to a standstill quite early on, and with no sobbing relatives willing to admit any kinship to him for long enough to spurn the police on, his death and life were forgotten.

Angus settled back into his life, doing decorating jobs, selling ice cream and molesting children until the 70s came to a quiet end. It was almost 1980 when the police showed up on his doorstep with a warrant for his arrest. Angus went quietly, saying nothing until he could ascertain just how much the police knew. He had learned his lessons well after his first trial. The key to surviving an interrogation was to know what was on the table before you said anything. Angus sat with his arms sullenly crossed and his mouth shut as the police railed at him. He sat in absolute silence for almost an hour until he was certain of what he was being arrested for, then he made a full confession. The man who had sold him the gun had been arrested and turned over his client list in exchange for a lenient sentence. The police retrieved the weapon from his recently refurbished campervan without giving anything else a second look and sent him off to jail for illegal possession of a firearm with barely a complaint from any of the parties involved. Angus was given a few minutes to calmly explain to his wife that he had made a mistake, Sarah accepted the apology at face value and tearfully promised to wait for his return. There were no real repercussions for Angus: his family had savings that would cover his six-month sentence, and while the number of reported rapes and molestations in Glasgow dropped, there was still enough baseline evil at work that his contributions were not noticed. His imprisonment couldn't have been comfortable, but he was an adult with a penchant for violence now instead of a frightened child, and whatever reputation had preceded him last time was now long forgotten.

By the middle of 1980, Angus was back on the streets of Glasgow and back to his old tricks. He put down a £3000 deposit on one of the newly built houses in a new estate in South Nitshill and got back into his usual routines without missing a step. By June of 1982, he was starting to get sloppy as his old desires crept back up on him and the police showed no signs of even looking for him. He lured a girl into a close in the Govanhill estate but when she saw him coming in after her, she ran away screaming, realising what was happening from the stories that had been shared around the neighbourhood. Later the same day he managed to corner a seven-year-old girl in a swimsuit in another close in nearby Patrick. She did not get away unscathed but her sobbing report was added to the growing list of cases that the local police were linking together into a pattern.

Later that month a girl of just six years old was dragged into a close and raped in the Woodlands area of the city. Her testimony was added to the mounting evidence. She vividly remembered that the man who had pinned her face-down on the cold concrete floor had green paint splattered across his shoes. Another raped girl came forward with additional details months after her initial interview, in an art class she had caught a whiff of turpentine and started sobbing uncontrollably because that smell had clung to her attacker. Another victim corroborated the detail of the smell when she was given the opportunity, and the police realised that the odd outfit that the man had been described as wearing could have belonged to a painter or decorator. With that connecting evidence and a pool of offenders to winnow through the police began to retrace their steps, showing each victim photographs including the one taken during Angus' last prison stay. All in all, twelve separate girls picked Angus out as their attacker.

When the police arrived on his doorstep this time they saw that he had a child in the house and informed Sarah of the crimes that he was being charged with. He had no opportunity to put a spin on events, no chance to twist things around so that he was the wounded party. Sarah knew him in that moment in a way that she had not known him throughout their entire marriage. Angus was led away in handcuffs for the second time in less than a year.

This time the interrogators were ready for Angus to stonewall them the way that he had in previous investigations, so they quickly laid out the details of every crime and started pressing him to present an alternate version of events if he was truly innocent. Time and practice had sharpened Angus' wits and ability to lie on his feet. He outright denied every single crime and began fabricating excuse after excuse and alibi after alibi for as long as they were questioning him. He never tripped over his own lies and before long the police were as confused and angry as Angus was pretending to be. They took a break to get coffee and found that Sarah had arrived at the station. With few better ideas, they let her in to talk to Angus, although they left their recording equipment turned on. She settled into the seat opposite him and asked, 'Did you do it?'

'No. Of course not. How could you think…'

She cut him off. 'How many of them? How many times did you do it?'

Angus fell into sullen silence. Sarah set her jaw. 'You are going to admit what you've done. You're not going to drag this family through a court case. You're not going to drag all those kiddies into court to point at you and say you did it. Just admit it. Admit it you coward.'

Angus refused to meet her eyes, but he mumbled, 'Alright.'

When the police returned to the room, Angus was suddenly a lot more forthcoming. 'I was lying before. I did it. I did all of it. I've lost count of how many times I've done it. I've done so many of them that I can't remember all that I've done. If you can find out when and where, I'll tell you if I did them or not. Is that fair?'

Angus Sinclair was convicted on three counts of rape and nine counts of sexual assault in 1982. Lord Cameron, the judge of his case, had to decide on his sentencing. He told Sinclair, 'The penalty for rape is entirely discretionary and without limit. I have considered very carefully whether a limit should be placed on the extent of the penalty, and I have decided there is only one limit—namely your life.'

Life sentences for rape were rare in Scotland at the time, but due to the vile nature of Angus' crimes and the sheer volume of offences that he had committed, it seemed like the only viable solution. It was only after the case was settled that the full details of Angus earlier murder and molestation charges came to light, ratifying the judge's decision to remove him from society. Angus was sent to Peterhead prison, where his mother, sister and niece took several buses to come and visit him as often as they were allowed. Despite everything, they stood by their monster. Sarah never spoke to Angus again. Not even to file for divorce. Legally the two are still married.

Cold Cases

Angus settled back into prison life without much difficulty and the years began to roll by. His life was completely stagnant and unchanging, but outside the walls of Peterhead prison, the world was changing rapidly. With the passing years came new technologies and advances in crime detection, but the most important change in the world outside was that the police now knew about Angus. They understood his dark motivations and the depths of depravity that he would descend to if it would satisfy his urges. They began to backtrack through his history and tried to connect him with other crimes.

While Sarah would no longer speak to Angus, she was happy to speak to the police, and they took her on a long tour of various crime scenes that they suspected were the work of

Angus. Each time, she was easily able to pinpoint the connection to Angus. Some women had been abducted within spitting distance of their family home at the time. Some children had been molested near to Angus' usual haunts. Even this horrible experience gradually became routine as the cold case team would come to collect Sarah and then drop her off again in tears. The police were then tasked with finding enough evidence beyond the circumstantial connections between Angus and the crime scenes—something that proved considerably more difficult.

DNA identification was still in its early days in the 80s and it was poorly understood. Angus, in particular, didn't know what he was agreeing to when he volunteered his DNA sample for comparison to crime scenes as a means of getting the police to stop badgering him with questions. A single hair had been found on the body of his final victim, Mary Gallacher, and when it was run through the tests it came up as a perfect match for Angus. He was tried and convicted, while still denying everything, and murder was the final straw for his sister and niece. Maimie didn't believe for an instant that her boy could have been capable of killing someone. Just as she hadn't been able to believe that his first murder, back when he was a teenager, had been anything but an accident. She went on believing that he was innocent until her quiet death at home in 1987. Not long afterwards, Sarah left Scotland, never to return; all obligations to her husband, real or imagined, had long been fulfilled. Sentencing was slower this time, ending in an additional life sentence strapped on to the end of his existing one. Any faint possibility that Angus Sinclair would ever roam free again vanished permanently.

The World's End murders still haunted the public consciousness, even decades after they had been committed. They were a stain on the record of the Scottish police, too, so when they believed that technology had advanced sufficiently, the cold case was reopened by a special team known as 'Operation Trinity.' Lester Knibb, the technician who had first examined the forensic evidence from the World's End killings, made a long journey down to a lab in England with the materials that he had carefully preserved through all the years, and two sets of DNA were discovered on the clothing of the girls. The DNA of the men found on both of the girls was compared to swabs taken from the 500 subjects that were originally suspected of committing the crimes. There was no match found.

Still, the world refused to forget about Christine Eadie and Helen Scott. Their families were still demanding justice and interest in the case only seemed to build after decades of silence. With the DNA sample that the police had acquired from the bodies, they would be able to secure a conviction as soon as the perpetrator was found, and they had already eliminated 500 of the most likely perpetrators in one fell swoop. Information about the crime began to be circulated again and the timelines of known killers began getting compared to the date and location of their death. Still, nothing came up for years. The cold case team began to despair until the media intervened in an unexpected way. The long-running British show Crimewatch showed a reconstruction of the events that led to the deaths of the girls at the World's End pub and hammered the date of the killings back into the mind of the public, and like magic, the phone began to ring. In the weeks following the broadcast, the police received over a hundred and thirty calls from witnesses to the events that were being described, along with a few outlying calls from people who had not realised the significance of what they had seen on that night until a narrative was presented to them. A man who had been out walking by Gosford Bay on the night of the murders had seen what he once thought was a works van being driven erratically. A works van that he now suspected might have been a campervan. More details emerged from the witness statements that finally helped to clarify the events of the night.

The timeline of the murders had been skewed because there were two separate pairs of girls in the World's End that night, wearing similar outfits and fitting similar descriptions. A solid half of the original statements that had been taken from the patrons in attendance had been describing the actions of the wrong duo. When the correct girls were identified, the description of the men who were with them began to become much clearer. One detail in particular, the strange workman's outfit that one of the supposed killers wore, rang an alarm bell in the back of the mind of one of the original investigators into the murder of Mary Gallacher. Angus Sinclair perfectly matched the description that witnesses were giving, and it was known that he had frequented the bars in Edinburgh at that time with his brother-in-law.

While these allegations were coming to light, the Lothian and Borders police reached out to the Forensic Science Service for help in identifying the unknown DNA sample that had been found on both of the girls. It produced a partial match with over 200 known offenders in the National DNA database.

Desperate to move forward, the cold case team pressed for conviction, retrieving Angus from his place in prison and charging him with the abduction, rape and murder of both girls. Two years later, in August of 2007, Angus finally stood trial for the World's End murders.

Trial and Jeopardy

As with his molestation charges, the presiding judge in the case was Lord Clarke, a man already predisposed to assume the absolute worst about Angus and to hand down the harshest possible punishments that the law would allow. With no woman in his life to force him to be truthful, Angus pleaded not guilty to all charges and then proceeded to enter two special defences. One of them stated that any sexual activity between him and the girls had been entirely consensual and the second alleged that any harm that had come to the girls had been inflicted on them by Gordon Hamilton, his brother-in-law.

The police had long suspected that there was more than one assailant involved in the case. While both of the girls had been bound at their hands and feet, the knots used on the girls were different from each other. When his name was presented, the police scrambled to find Gordon Hamilton, only to discover that he had died six years prior to the case coming to fruition. They collected DNA samples from Sarah and all of his other relatives to try to produce a conclusive match.

The trial began, with the eyewitness testimony about a 'works van' near to Gosford Bay being linked to Angus by one of the police officers who had investigated him on the stand. He had owned a Toyota Hiace caravanette at the time of the murders, and it was suspected to be both the scene of the crime and the getaway vehicle as well as the connection to the eyewitness testimony. The police had hunted for this campervan frantically in the years leading up to the trial only to discover that it had been destroyed in the late 90s along with all of the evidence that it contained.

Forensic experts took the stand, confirming that there were semen samples retrieved from within the two victims and that they believed those samples matched Angus Sinclair's profile and what they would have expected Gordon Hamilton's profile to look like, were he still alive.

Shortly afterwards, Angus' defence team put forward a submission that there was no case to answer. There was no evidence that the sexual contact he had with the two girls was not consensual and there was no evidence that he had been involved in any violent action against them. With no other evidence connecting Angus to the murders, the judge was forced to dismiss the charges.

In the aftermath of the trial, Angus' other crimes were revealed to the general public and there was an uproar. The police and the population at large were utterly convinced of his guilt, but under the law of the land, once a trial was completed there was no mechanism to try someone on the same charges again. The laws of double jeopardy had been on the books since time immemorial, and they protected men like Angus from being dragged back into court over and over on flimsy evidence. In short, the laws existed to ensure that the judiciary had their act together before they started accusing people of crimes, not after the trial had already begun.

The fury expressed in the press showed no signs of dying down any time soon, and before long the Lord Advocate of the judiciary was called on to address the Scottish Parliament on the matter of the case. Elish Angiolini had grown up in an area of Glasgow not far from the one where Angus Sinclair had committed his first crimes and took the role of Lord Advocate only after years working to improve the Scottish legal system. She announced to parliament that she was unhappy with the decision that Lord Clarke had made in this case. She firmly believed that the sparse evidence that was being presented by the court would have been enough to win over the jury in this case. This launched a political firefight between different members of the judiciary, with others accusing Angiolini of undermining public confidence in judges and others questioning whether decisions of the magnitude made by Lord Clarke should really fall to a single judge rather than a panel.

The end result of all of the noise being made was a complete overhaul of the Scottish legal system. Three separate amendments were made to criminal proceedings after all of the dust had settled.

The first change was that 'bad character' and similar evidence could now be entered into consideration in a trial, so a man standing accused of murder who was already a convicted murderer could be described as such without it being considered prejudicial to the case. This change opened up a legal can of worms that is still being untangled to this day, but it meant that prosecution of repeat offenders became much easier.

The second change was that a mechanism was put into place for decisions made by trial judges to be appealed if enough of their peers felt that it was made in error. Lord Clarke's decision that there was insufficient evidence was cited as the main point of contention, but even so, this mechanism was not used to overturn that decision and bring Angus back to trial as it could only be applied to future cases once the law was passed.

The final change to the legal system did away with the concept of double jeopardy. There were high standards required to reopen a case: new and compelling evidence had to be produced by the police before the courts would undertake a second trial. With that new goal in mind, the cold case team dove back into their work.

They had discovered traces of DNA on the ligatures used to bind and choke the girls, but over the years it had badly degraded to the point that it was useless in the first trial. New technologies had been developed in the intervening years and a local biotech firm came forward to help piece the DNA profile from the two distinct sets of knots together. One of the profiles was a positive match for Angus Sinclair and the other matched with what they suspected was Gordon Hamilton, but the police still did not have a direct reference to prove it, so they turned to the cold case team for help and were amazed at the results.

Since preparation for the trial began, the cold case team had been working tirelessly to rebuild the timeline of Angus Sinclair and Gordon Hamilton's whereabouts throughout the years. It was well known that the two of them were friends and it was a poorly kept secret that they went out trawling for women when they were meant to be on their 'fishing trips' every other weekend, but what was less well known was the fact that Angus had taken on Gordon as an apprentice to his painting and decorating business for a while when business was booming and the younger man was out of work. The cold case team had managed to identify the homes that the two of them had worked in, and with the consent of the homeowners and the help of the forensics team, they removed some plastering work that Gordon had performed to discover one of his hairs trapped behind it and perfectly preserved. It gave an equally perfect match to the second set of DNA. They had sufficient evidence to bring Angus back on trial for the murders, and with the evidence from the ligatures, they could prove that he was involved in the violence, too.

Three judges deliberated on whether the evidence was sufficient to overlook the existing rules of double jeopardy and concluded that it was, and a second trial date was set in 2014. Angus still denied all of his actions, entering three special defences this time: that his sexual encounter with the girls had been consensual, that Gordon Hamilton had committed the crimes without his knowledge, and that he had an alibi. The same lie about a fishing trip that he had fed to his wife was regurgitated verbatim in a court of law, and despite having no corroborating witnesses, Angus somehow thought that it was going to hold up.

The evidence was presented to the jury methodically over the course of several days, with Angus' lawyer trying desperately to find a single fault in the narrative that the prosecutors were presenting. At one point the jury was driven out to visit the scene of the crime and have the events of the murder narrated to them by the prosecutors. The jury deliberated for only minutes after all evidence had been presented before returning their verdict that Angus was guilty of the murders. He was sentenced to yet another lifetime of imprisonment. He will become eligible for parole at the ripe old age of 106.

Conclusion

Angus Sinclair spends his time in bed or in his prison-issued wheelchair in Glenochil prison, Clackmannanshire. He will be lucky to survive the rest of the year after a series of strokes. He has gone from the haggard look that followed him through his last public appearances at the trial to appearing skeletal. His eyes are sunken into his head, but they still hold the spark of malice as they roll around to track anyone walking by. He has an emergency alert tied to his wrist in case he falls, and the prison staff dutifully care for him as they wait for him to die. He drinks from a sealed baby cup—the only source of nutrition available to him as he struggles to eat the restricted diet that the prison doctors have put him on. He cannot make the trip from his bed to the toilet in the corner of his cell unaided. He cannot change his own clothes. The man who was once so obsessed with power and control over the people around him has now been left unable to even control his own bowels. Age has stripped him of everything that he thought made him special.

The staff in the prison are mindful of their duty of care. They do not make him wait when he needs assistance, they treat him better than many sullen and silent old men in nursing homes are treated, but they are aware of who and what he is. They offer him no kindness beyond what is legally obliged of them. He will never see another smile. He will never hear another joke. He is dead in every way except for the fact that his heart is still beating, and his malevolent intelligence is still working away behind his expressionless face.

His family and friends have all forgotten and abandoned him, his wife has moved on to a new life, his son has changed his name so that he cannot be linked to his monstrous father. The only people still trying to draw sound out of his lapsing throat are the old policemen who come to visit, hoping that in what are clearly his final months on this earth, he might suddenly develop enough of a conscience to set some grieving family's minds at rest. To date, Angus Sinclair has only been officially tried for four murders, including the one he committed as a teenager. The vast majority of his crimes remain unanswered due to a lack of surviving evidence.

The only way that the families of Frances Barker, Anna Kenny, Hilda McAuley, Agnes Cooney and Eddie Cotogno are ever going to know for certain what happened to their beloved daughters, sisters, and brother is if Angus confesses to his crimes. Of course, he will not do it because there is no advantage to him in admitting to more murders. Every word he speaks takes a great deal of effort after the strokes, and he certainly isn't going to waste that effort on other people. He is a classic sociopath. A sadistic sexually motivated killer with no interest in anything except his own hedonistic pleasure.

At one point during the investigation into the World's End murders, the police brought in an FBI profiler to assist them, and the pattern that profiler described was that of a classic serial killer. Someone who is incapable of empathy, interested only in what they can take from the world. A person not only devoid of empathy but aroused by fear and pain. At a very early age Angus Sinclair became obsessed with sex, and due to his poor social skills, he had no way to pursue it, so instead, he turned to rape and molestation. At that age, sexual encounters are formative experiences. He remained obsessed with sex, but for him, sex was no longer the consensual act between two lovers—it was an act of violence, and the more violent the act could be made, the more pleasurable it became for him. The wires in his brain got crossed and once he made that association there was no turning back. In the beginning, he may have killed as a means to cover up his crimes, but before long the killing was an end in itself. He revelled in murder and he drew joy from the painful death of his victims.

In the lifespan of most serial killers we see a pattern of escalation, where they go from one killing every few years to one every month, to a final berserk stage where they are killing every moment that they can, when they believe that they have become impossible to stop and there is no reason to restrain themselves. In Angus Sinclair's case, that escalation happened within a seven-month period during which he committed almost all of his murders. It is for the best that he lacked the confidence of his kind, that Mary Gallacher fought back against him so valiantly that he was too frightened to go out hunting for more victims and that he was so cowed by just the memory of her that he could not bring himself to kill again.

The families of the World's End murder victims feel no sorrow to hear that Angus Sinclair is on death's door. They feel no sympathy for him and their only wish is that he had died a long time ago before he could inflict his own personal brand of evil on the world. Still, even they have asked him to reveal his secrets so that the other families of his victims will know peace. It grows less likely with each passing day, as his muscles weaken and the likelihood of one final stroke finishing him off grows.

The total death toll of Angus Sinclair's campaign of terror will probably never be known. Even this book only recounts the cases for which enough information has been gathered for us to make reasonable suppositions. Any time that he went beyond his usual hunting grounds or murdered with different methods will have gone unnoticed. The full number of children that he molested and raped has never come to light, although the crime statistics for Glasgow showed a fairly significant drop after he was incarcerated. Soon he will be dead, and with him will go the only full record of the murders that he has committed and the children whose innocence he destroyed. Even in death, he will continue his legacy of misery: a trail of weeping families whose lives he has utterly ruined in the pursuit of his sick pleasure, his own family included in that number.

About the Author

Ryan Green is an author and freelance writer in his late thirties. He lives in Herefordshire, England with his wife, three children and two dogs. Outside of writing and spending time with his family, Ryan enjoys walking, reading and wind surfing.

Ryan is fascinated with History, Psychology, True Crime, Serial Killers and Organised Crime. In 2015, he finally started researching and writing his own work and at the end of the year he released his first book on Britain's most notorious serial killer – Harold Shipman.

His books are packed with facts, alternative considerations, and open mindedness. Ryan puts the reader in the perspective of those who lived and worked in proximity of his subjects.

Other Titles by Ryan Green

If you enjoyed reading *Sinclair* you may like these other titles by Ryan Green:

Harold Shipman: The True Story of Britain's Most Notorious Serial Killer

Colombian Killers: The True Stories of the Three Most Prolific Serial Killers on Earth

Fred & Rose West: Britain's Most Infamous Killer Couples

The Kuřim Case: A Terrifying True Story of Child Abuse, Cults & Cannibalism

Obeying Evil: The Mockingbird Hill Massacre Through the Eyes of a Killer

The Truro Murders: The Sex Killing Spree Through the Eyes of an Accomplice

Printed in Great
Britain
by Amazon